Colonial Women

ALSO BY CAROLE CHANDLER WALDRUP

Presidents' Wives: The Lives of
44 American Women of Strength
(McFarland, 1989)

The Vice Presidents: Biographies of the
45 Men Who Have Held the
Second Highest Office in the United States
(McFarland, 1996)

Colonial Women

23 Europeans Who Helped Build a Nation

by
CAROLE CHANDLER WALDRUP

McFarland & Company, Inc., Publishers
Jefferson, North Carolina, and London

Library of Congress Cataloguing-in-Publication Data

Waldrup, Carole Chandler, 1925–
        Colonial women : 23 Europeans who helped build a nation /
by Carole Chandler Waldrup.
        p.   cm.
        Includes bibliographical references and index.
        ISBN 0-7864-0664-X (sewn softcover : 50# alkaline paper) ∞
        1. United States — History — Colonial period, ca. 1600–
1775 Biography.   2. Women — United States Biography.
3. European Americans Biography.   I. Title.
        E187.5.W35   1999
        920.72'0973'09032 — dc21   99-32056
                                                                          CIP

British Library Cataloguing-in-Publication data are available

Manufactured in the United States of America

McFarland & Company, Inc., Publishers
    Box 611, Jefferson, North Carolina 28640
    www.mcfarlandpub.com

To my favorite in-laws,
Margaret R. Waldrup and
John H. Speagle

Table of Contents

Table of Contents

Introduction

The first women who came to America can accurately be described as brave heroines. They faced life in a wilderness with nothing to use in their housekeeping but their own two hands, a knife or two, some iron pots in the kitchen, wooden bowls, and straw-filled bags that served as beds.

They gave birth to their children with only the assistance of another woman, contracted illnesses for which there was no cure and, with mud-daubed wooden chimneys on their houses, faced the ever-present danger of fire.

As someone said, "This was a great country for men and dogs, but it was tough on women and horses."

Each woman profiled in this book was born and grew up in a European country. Each came to the New World hoping to find a better life, either in terms of religious freedom or financial improvement. None came with a guarantee she would realize her dream.

They came with no civil rights because they were women, but gradually their lot improved. By the time of the Revolutionary War, women were working at jobs outside their homes and had gained some legal control over their possessions.

We owe these women more than we realize. If they had not been willing to endure endless hardship, male colonists might not have remained long in America.

1

Priscilla Mullins Alden

Priscilla Mullins was one of the passengers on the *Mayflower* when it arrived at Plymouth Rock in 1620, and she was one of the few women who survived the first year there. In fact, she lived for many more years and was a witness to much development of the Massachusetts Bay area.

Priscilla was born about 1602 in Dorking, Surrey, England, about 30 miles southwest of London. Her parents, William and Alice Mullins, or "Molines" as her father signed his name, may have been French Huguenots, but this has never been verified.

For at least two generations, the Mullins family had lived in the Dorking area, where Priscilla's father was a boot and shoe merchant. When he learned, earlier in 1620, of the planned migration of English citizens to the New World, he decided to emigrate with his wife and two youngest children, Priscilla, then 18 years old, and Joseph, about seven years old. Two older Mullins children were grown, married and living in their own homes.

Economic conditions in England had not been good for some time and were growing worse. Mr. Mullins believed the market for the footwear he sold would be better among the colonists, since few, if any, shoe shops would be available there. The Virginia colony, where the Mullins were bound, had been settled since 1608, and no doubt some of the colonists needed new shoes.

At first there were two ships sailing to the New World. On one were passengers who had embarked from Leyden, Holland, where they had been living for the past several years as refugees from English religious persecution. Their ship was called the *Speedwell*, and these people wanted to put more distance between themselves and their English tormentors.

Waiting for the *Speedwell* at Southampton, England, was captain Christopher Jones, the master of the *Mayflower*. The passengers aboard Jones' ship were not leaving England primarily for religious reasons, but rather because they believed they would prosper financially in the new colony.

At Southampton, it was decided the *Mayflower* would carry all the passengers, with the *Speedwell* carrying the supplies of food, tools and household furnishings of the colonists. After two false starts, however, it became evident that the *Speedwell* was not seaworthy.

All the passengers and all their possessions were then loaded onto the *Mayflower*, and since there were 102 passengers and about 30 crewmen occupying the small ship, some supplies and household furnishing had to be left behind.

On board the ship, there was only room for each passenger to have an area the size of a single bed below the upper deck. In this small, dark, smelly space, Priscilla and her family, as well as other passengers, lived for the next 63 days. Sanitary facilities consisted of buckets that were emptied overboard.

The food available was salted meat, hardened cheese and flat crackers, with beer or wine to drink. Due to frequent stormy weather, it was impossible to cook most of the time because of the danger that sparks from open fires in the galley might ignite flammable materials on the ship.

The crossing was rough, and most of the passengers became seasick. When the ship encountered winter storms in November, the waves were so high and turbulence so severe, mothers were forced to tie their small children to their bunks or other fixed objects on the ship to prevent injuries.

A passenger, Mrs. Elizabeth Hopkins, gave birth to a son while the ship was still at sea. She and her husband named the child, appropriately, Oceanus.

At long last, land was sighted. To the surprise of the passengers, their ship was nowhere near Virginia, their expected destination. Instead, they were several hundred miles farther north, Massachusetts, in what would be known later as the Cape Cod area.

The passengers from the London region knew this change in the location of a new settlement would mean the English government would have no real control over their colony. According to William Bradford's record of events in his journal, these Londoners said they would "use their own liberty; for none had power to command them."

These reckless words alarmed the leaders of the colonists, who knew law and order in the new settlement could be observed only by the consent of the people themselves. There was no police force, militia or other enforcement agency to keep order.

It was at this time the leaders wrote the Mayflower Compact, which set out rules and regulations to be observed by all present and future citizens of the colony and gave the colonists the right to vote for a governor to lead them. Only men would have the right to vote.

The Compact said:

> In the name of God, Amen. We whose names are underwritten, the loyal subjects of our dread Sovereign Lord King James, by the grace of God of Great Britain, France and Ireland King, defender of the faith, etc.
>
> Having undertaken, for the Glory of God, and advancement of the Christian faith and Honor of our King and Country, a Voyage to plant the First Colony in the Northern Parts of Virginia, do by these presents solemnly and mutually in the presence of God and one of another, Covenant and Combine ourselves together into a Civil Body Politic, for our better ordering and preservation and furtherance of the ends aforesaid; and by virtue hereof to enact, constitute and frame such

just and equal Laws, Ordinances, Acts, Constitutions and Offices from time to time, as shall be thought most meet and convenient for the general good of the Colony, unto which we promise all due submission and obedience. In witness whereof, we have hereunder subscribed our names at Cape Cod, the 11th of November, in the year of the reign of our Sovereign Lord King James of England, France and Ireland the eighteenth, and of Scotland the fifty-fourth. Anno Domino. 1620.

Priscilla's father and all the other men, except servants, signed that they would be bound by the Compact and the *Mayflower* pulled into shore on December 21, 1620, at what would someday become the state of Massachusetts.

The immediate view the *Mayflower* passengers had of their new home was not promising. As William Bradford wrote, "What could they see but a hideous and desolate wilderness, full of wild beasts and wild men? And what multitudes there might be of them, they knew not.... For summer, being done all things stand upon them with a weather-beaten face; and the whole country, full of woods and thickets, represented a wild and savage view...."

The men formed an exploration group to examine the new territory, while Priscilla, her mother and the other women went ashore to wash all the dirty clothes that had accumulated during the two-month voyage. Two dogs had accompanied the *Mayflower* passengers, a mastiff and a spaniel, and while the women did the laundry, the children ran and played on the beach.

After the men decided on a location for the new colony, to be called Plymouth, the cannons and cannon balls were moved to the highest hill overlooking the site. They determined their next project would be the construction of a large common house, which would serve as a temporary shelter for the men while they built houses for their families and would later be used for religious services and other town meetings and social gatherings.

One of the men involved in the construction of the common house was a young man named John Alden. He had sailed out of London when the Mullins family did and had also come to the New World for an opportunity to earn a better living.

John was a barrel-maker by trade. The financial backers of the Plymouth colony had hired Alden to come with the others because his woodworking abilities would be of great importance to the colony. He had promised he would stay for at least a year and would assist the colonists with their house building, barrel-making and furniture construction.

No doubt John and Priscilla were acquainted with each other from having sailed for so many days in close quarters, but at that time they had other concerns than romance.

The common house was finally completed after about two weeks of tiring, heavy labor — chopping down trees, cutting away limbs and dressing out framing as best they could with few tools available. The walls were made of matted, woven vines, liberally daubed with mud, and the roof was steep and covered with thatch made of reeds.

When it was finished, most of the men went to live in it, while the women and children remained on the ship. Captain Jones had told them they could remain on the *Mayflower* while the men built houses. He and his crew had no plans to try to recross the Atlantic Ocean during winter weather.

Most of the men worked enthusiastically, even on Christmas Day, 1620. The Puritan colonists who had sailed from Holland did not believe Christmas should be celebrated except with sermons and prayers, as they could find no basis for any other celebration in the Scriptures.

There was some unhappy muttering among the Londoners about the lack of celebration. Their view was that if these strange pilgrims from Holland wanted to ignore Christmas as "a survival of heathen ways," it was their privilege. The others wanted to celebrate Christmas.

Captain Jones must have been among the latter group, as he brought out a special keg of beer on Christmas Day and served it to all who wanted to drink it. That constituted the festivities.

During the winter days, the weather turned bitterly cold with sleet falling, then snow and then sleet; many of the men became ill. All the passengers had been weakened by the weeks of deprivation, and disease soon spread to the women and children, as well as to the *Mayflower* crew.

People began dying from their illnesses, and the deaths continued until only 50 colonists and about 15 sailors were still living, including Captain Jones. Only four wives and seven girls were still alive.

Priscilla lost both her parents and her little brother. She must have been terrified when she considered her future living alone in such bleak surroundings. She had inherited a supply of 40 assorted pairs of shoes and boots and the equivalent of $100 (in today's currency) in a will made by her father in February, 1621, so she was not completely destitute.

The *Mayflower* returned to England when the weather improved, and the women and children moved into the crude homes the men had built.

The cannons and ammunition had been placed on the top floor of the common house, and religious services were held regularly in the room below. Services were led by an older man named William Brewster, who had been one of the religious leaders in Leyden.

William and his wife, Mary Brewster, asked Priscilla to come live with them after her family died. She was glad to join their household, which consisted of William, Mary and their two sons, Love and Wrestling.

Before many months, Priscilla had a proposal of marriage from Captain Miles Standish, or so legend says. The captain was a former member of the British Army stationed in Holland during the time some of the Plymouth colonists lived there, and he had been charged with defense of Plymouth colony. His wife had died during the epidemic.

As Captain Standish was too shy to propose to Priscilla on his own behalf, he asked John Alden to speak for him. To John's surprise and delight, Priscilla asked him why he did not ask for himself. John Alden was described as a man of most excellent form with a fair and ruddy complexion. He was about 22 years old at the time of the proposal.

Priscilla married John Alden sometime in 1622 and they set up their own household.

The houses of the settlers were crude and small, built in the same manner as the common house with wood framing and mud-daubed walls, chimneys were made either of wood, caked with mud inside, or of rocks held together with mud. The only outside light entered the homes through small slits cut in the door and covered with oiled paper.

Priscilla and the other women cooked meals over open hearth fires using heavy iron cooking pots with long handles so the housewife could change the position of utensils hanging over the open fire and not be burned. Some foods were cooked by being covered with hot coals.

Often there was not enough food, and the colonists had either to buy corn from nearby Indians or ration the supply of food they had. Their financial backers in England were slow in responding to requests for further assistance.

Indians taught the colonists how to plant and cook maize. They boiled young, tender ears of the corn in hot water in summer and ground dried kernels into a powder-like substance in a mill made from a log about three feet long, hollowed out about half way down, and used a sturdy wooden stick to pound the kernels into fine particles for use in porridges and bread.

The Indians were friendly with the colonists and often came in large groups to visit Plymouth. Plymouth officials declared a day of thanksgiving after the first corn crop was harvested, and the Indians were invited as honored guests at a Thanksgiving feast.

Priscilla and John probably used long wooden trough-like bowls, called trenchers, from which to serve food and eat. The trenchers were oblong or square, and the diners ate with their hands, two or more people dipping and eating from the same trencher. Plainly, napkins were necessary, and each housewife had an ample supply.

There were a few wooden mugs in each household for beverages, usually spring water in Plymouth. These were passed around among the diners as needed.

In earliest Plymouth all the land was owned in common, but in 1623 the cleared land was divided among the settlers, and their houses and lots became their own, giving them an incentive to work harder and make the colony strong and successful.

John Alden received an acre of land for himself and one for Priscilla also, giving them enough space to grow their own food.

Later that year, more Separatists left Holland to come to live in Plymouth. The newcomers were welcomed heartily, since they brought news of friends and relatives in England and Holland.

While John, Priscilla and the other citizens of Plymouth were proud of the progress they had made in carving a colony out of the wilderness, the newest arrivals were appalled by the living conditions of the residents.

The newcomers, having recently lived in a busy, noisy, prosperous Dutch town, expected to find an organized, functioning village. Instead they found people wearing ragged, worn clothing, living in the poorest type of houses, with only fish and wild game to eat until the next corn crop was harvested. Fortunately, the newcomers had brought food supplies with them.

The surrounding countryside was daunting. Wolves howled in the dense forest at night, and a constant watch was needed to prevent injuries from wild animals invading the village during the day. When they walked to springs to dip water into their jugs, often a silent, painted Indian brave stepped out of the bushes along the path and watched the settlers. An overriding fear was of a raid and possible massacre by hostile Indians.

The English sponsors of Plymouth were beginning to realize that their dreams of riches from fishing and fur trading by the settlers were overly optimistic, as months passed and no profits were seen. Some members of the sponsoring group withdrew their support entirely, and Plymouth officials were told that the total indebtedness of the colony was an amount equal to $70,000 (by present day calculations)!

The disappointed sponsors said they expected the colonists to stop spending their time "in idleness and talking." Plainly, the sponsors had no concept of how difficult life was in Plymouth. John Alden and several of the other men decided they would pay off their sponsors. They formed a group called Undertakers and using boats belonging to the Plymouth colony, began trading with the Indians.

All Plymouth residents were required to pay three bushels of corn or six pounds of tobacco for each family member per year. These payments were for their houses and lots; in turn, the Undertakers would furnish residents with the equivalent of $250 in shoes and hose each year in exchange for corn at six shillings a bushel. These shoes and hose were to be divided among the settlers.

By 1627 Priscilla and John had two children named Elizabeth and John. Other families were growing also and the total population of Plymouth stood at 180 people.

Homes began to improve in both size and quality as the men had more time to properly prepare boards for building. John Alden made furniture for those needing it, although a few of the later arrivals brought some furniture with them. Glass windows began to appear in newer houses.

Priscilla still had to make her own soap from household cooking grease and wood ashes, and she dipped her family's candles from animal tallow rendered in cooking. She added bayberry juice to both soap and candles to give them a nice odor.

She and other housewives allowed laundry to accumulate for at least a month before washing it outside in boiling water, which was in an iron washpot over an open fire. Extreme weather sometimes delayed washdays for several weeks. The clean, rinsed clothes were spread out on bushes to dry.

Plymouth officials passed a law requiring every resident to attend religious services, still held in the common house. On Sunday mornings they marched solemnly, three abreast, to church. While neither John nor Priscilla had come to Plymouth for religious reasons, they eagerly embraced the beliefs and practices of their neighbors and friends.

Men and boys sat on one side of the meeting room, with women and girls on the other, to listen to sermons usually lasting three to four hours! A tithing man was selected by church leaders to watch worshippers during the service to make sure no one went to sleep. In his hand he carried a long rod which had a foxtail fastened to one end and a wooden knob on the other. If Priscilla or another female dozed, their faces were tickled with the foxtail. If John or other males napped, they received a sharp rap on their head from the wooden knob.

The meeting room was not heated in winter; perhaps the tithing man may have wanted to be sure the sleepers had not frozen to death in the cold Massachusetts winter weather!

Other smaller colonies started appearing in the general area of Plymouth, and settlers of these villages wanted to trade with the Indians for profit.

In 1628, the Plymouth Undertakers established a trading post on the banks of the Kennebec River, now the city of Augusta, Maine. They traded successfully with the Abnaki Indians for their beaver, otter and other furs in exchange for blankets, clothing and food items.

The venture was so successful, a man named Hocking, who was from a nearby colony, decided to establish a trading post of his own and was soon in business.

The assistant governor of Plymouth, John Howland, ordered Mr.

Hocking to leave, and John Alden, also an assistant governor, agreed that Hocking was trespassing.

Hocking refused to budge, and Howland sent two Plymouth residents out in a canoe to cut the anchoring cables on Hocking's boat. Freed of its anchor, the boat swung around, and as it did so, Hocking shot and killed one of the cable cutters, Moses Talbot. Talbot's companion then shot and killed Hocking.

When John Alden docked his trading vessel at Boston a few days later, he was arrested for Hocking's murder. Captain Standish was sent to Boston hastily to get Alden released, but Alden had to stand trial before the General Court there. He was found innocent, however, and was released.

By 1632, Plymouth was becoming crowded, and thousands of acres surrounding the town were meted out to citizens for use in farming or building. John and Priscilla were allotted a large tract about 10 miles north of Plymouth. They and their five children moved there as soon as John got another house built. Young John and Elizabeth Alden had been joined by sister Sarah and brothers Joseph and David.

Other families soon moved from Plymouth to live on newly acquired property.

John Alden always maintained his political ties with Plymouth's town government, and he served in various ways for about 55 years. He and Priscilla brought their children back to religious services in Plymouth at first, but it soon became a hardship, as they had to travel the 20 miles round trip either by oxcart or boat. In winter either mode of transportation was frequently impossible.

In 1637, John and Priscilla joined with their neighbors to request permission from Plymouth church officials to establish a religious group in their new location, called Duxbury. Permission was granted.

The Alden family continued to grow and prosper in Duxbury, and five more children were born — Mary, young Priscilla, Rebecca, Ruth and Jonathan.

Even though they had a real financial struggle lasting many years, John Alden paid off his share of indebtedness to Plymouth's English sponsors.

After she reached adulthood, young Elizabeth Alden married a farmer named William Pabodie. They moved to Rhode Island, where she lived to be 93 years old.

Young John Alden became a sea captain and was accused of witchcraft in Salem in 1692. If he had not escaped from jail, he might have been hanged.

Joseph and David Alden both became farmers in the nearby countryside. Their younger brother, Jonathan, farmed the Duxbury homestead with his father, and he helped his father build a new house in 1653.

Mary and young Priscilla Alden never married. Rebecca married Thomas Delano, and Sarah married Alexander Standish, son of Captain Miles Standish and his second wife. Ruth Alden married John Bass, a cartwheel maker and repairer from the Braintree area, and future presidents John Adams and son John Quincy Adams would be counted among her descendants.

Priscilla and John spent their declining years in the newer, larger house Jonathan had helped build, and they probably died there. Priscilla died sometime around 1682, and John died on September 12, 1687. They had been married for about 60 years! They were buried side by side on their farm near Eagle Tree Pond in Duxbury.

John Alden was the last survivor of the signers of the Mayflower Compact.

Bibliography

Langdon, George D., Jr. *Pilgrim Colony: A History of New Plymouth*. New Haven, Conn.: Yale University Press, 1966.

Williams, Alicia Crane. "John and Priscilla: We Hardly Knew Ye." *American History Magazine* 23, no. 6 (1988): 42–46.

Willison, George F. *Saints and Strangers*. New York: Time, 1964.

2

Alice Carpenter Southworth Bradford

In August 1623, the ship *Anne* and sister ship *Little James* sailed into Plymouth harbor, bringing a total of 93 more settlers to the colony. Among these new arrivals was Alice Carpenter Southworth, widow of Edward Southworth, a silkworker in Leyden, Holland, where they had lived as members of the original Separatist group from England.

Alice's sister, Juliana Morton, accompanied Alice, along with Juliana's husband, George, their four children and a nephew. Alice and Juliana had a sister named Priscilla Wright already living in Plymouth. Priscilla had emigrated to Plymouth with her husband, William, and one child in November 1621.

Alice Carpenter was born about 1590 to Alexander Carpenter and his wife in Wrington, Somersetshire, in England. Her father was a member of a dissenting sect called the Ancient Brethren. Alice married Edward Southworth in 1609 in Amsterdam, Holland, and had two sons, Constant and Thomas, who did not travel to Plymouth with her.

In all, 29 former members of the Leyden church congregation were on the ships most recently arrived, but their beloved pastor, John Robinson, was not one of them. Even though the sponsors of the Plymouth colony promised repeatedly they would send Robinson to Plymouth, he never came.

The newest arrivals at Plymouth were appalled by the primitive living conditions they found there. They had expected some semblance of an organized village; instead they found a vast, trackless wilderness, at the edge of which had been built several hutlike structures, a few better houses and two larger buildings.

Governor William Bradford wrote, "These passengers, when they saw their low and poor condition ashore were much daunted and dismayed, and according to their diverse humors were diversely affected; some wished themselves in England again; others fell aweeping, fancying their own misery in what they saw now in others."

The appearance of the original colonists was enough to daunt and dismay the most optimistic observer. Their clothes were ragged, the children, having grown, now wore whatever anyone else could give them. England seemed a long way off.

These new colonists had brought food supplies with them which was a great relief. It was decided by Governor Bradford and his assistants that these supplies should be shared by the newcomers, with the other settlers being fed from the harvest.

William Bradford, who was one of the original colonists of Plymouth, had been named to the office when their first governor, John Carver, died in 1621. Bradford was a reasonable, peace-loving man who had made great effort to be friendly to the Indians in the area, welcoming their advice and planting instructions. Their crops had done fairly well the first year, especially the Indian maize they planted, but the English barley, peas and wheat they had planted yielded almost nothing.

Chief Massasoit and 90 hungry Indian braves accepted the colonist's invitation to the first Thanksgiving feast. The men in Plymouth had shot some ducks and had seafood prepared to supplement the other food, but the women panicked when they saw so many additional hungry mouths to feed.

Apparently Chief Massasoit saw the colonists had not expected so many guests, so he sent some of his braves deer hunting. They brought back five deer, which helped the food supply last for the three days of celebrating, which included games of physical skill and strength, helping to forge a closer friendship with the Indians.

Governor Bradford's wife had died a few days after she had arrived in Plymouth with him, and he and Alice Southworth may have been corresponding. Whatever the circumstances, within a short time after her arrival in Plymouth, Alice married Bradford, whom she had known for years. He had worked with her husband in Leyden.

Alice married Bradford on August 14, 1623, and again the local Wampanoag Indians were guests at the wedding feast and celebration. Chief Massasoit and four other chiefs attended, bringing four buck deer and a wild turkey as gifts. One hundred twenty braves accompanied the chiefs.

Chief Massasoit was dressed in a black blanket, tied around his waist, and had a black wolf-skin cape thrown over his shoulders. He brought along only one of his wives, in deference to what he considered the strange customs of the white settlers.

Emmanuel Altham, captain of the *Little James*, and one of the wedding guests, wrote to his brother back in England about the wedding:

> We had about twelve pasty venisons, besides others, pieces of roasted venison and other such good cheer in such quantity that I could wish you some of our share. For here we have the best grapes that ever you saw — and the biggest, and diverse sorts of plums and nuts.

The Indians danced for the colonists after the ceremony.

Altham also mentioned there were now about 20 dwelling houses in Plymouth, "four or five of which are very fair and pleasant." He said the only livestock he saw were goats, pigs and chickens.

Governor Bradford had a substantial house where he and Alice began their life together. It was situated beside an intersection of two streets almost in the center of the village.

From his first marriage, Bradford had one son, John, born in 1615 and still living in Leyden with relatives.

Alice was wife of the governor, but she had to keep her household operating just as Priscilla Alden and the other women in Plymouth did. After her children were born, she was even busier.

William Bradford, Jr., was born in 1624, Mercy, in 1626, and Joseph, in 1628. Thomas and Constant Southworth came to live in Plymouth in 1628, and it must have been pleasing to Alice to have all of her family together. Young John Bradford had joined the household a year earlier, at age 12.

When the ship *Anne* returned to England, it was laden with a cargo of beaver and otter furs in addition to clapboard lumber, which could be sold for the profit of the colony's sponsors. Colonist Edward Winslow was a passenger on the *Anne* as a representative of Plymouth. He hoped to arrange sponsors to furnish supplies on a more regular basis and to obtain fishing equipment so that the colonists could become professional fishermen.

Governor Bradford was adamantly opposed to this venture as none of the colonists were fishermen by trade. He agreed, however, that they should try fishing to earn money to repay the sponsors.

Winslow returned to Plymouth in 1624 with some supplies but no luxuries. He did bring back three cows and a bull so the colonists could begin raising cattle for their own use.

Unfortunately, Winslow also brought bad news concerning future trading conditions. The supplies he had brought this trip would not be given to the colonists as before, but were to be sold at a price 40 percent higher than their cost in England! The furs and lumber the Plymouth people had sent would in the future be valued at 30 percent below real value to pay for its transport to England.

Governor Bradford and most of the other men felt the sponsors were taking unfair advantage of the colonists in their straitened circumstances, but believing they had no other choices, they agreed to comply with the new terms.

Plymouth law required all citizens to attend church services on Sunday, and everyone did, but they did not have a real minister for the first three years they lived in America. Ruling Elder William Brewster led Bible study and had requested permission to administer sacraments, but he was refused by officials in England. The men always carried their guns to church for protection against wild animals.

Minister John Lyford, a college graduate, accompanied Edward Winslow back to Plymouth to be the colony's religious leader. He appeared to be a humble, caring, honest man and the people were glad to have him join them.

They gave Lyford, his wife and five children the best house in Plymouth for their home, the largest food allotment possible and a servant. It became evident, however, that Lyford had many faults (one citizen referred to him as "unsavory salt"), and he and his family returned to England in 1624.

By the middle of 1626, the colonists had begun to feel they were gaining a little on the colossal debt to their sponsors when they managed to accumulate more furs than usual to pay on the debt.

Isaac Allerton, William Brewster's son-in-law, was sent along with the furs as a Plymouth agent to try to arrange yearly payments so Plymouth citizens could attain full ownership of the colony.

Allerton returned with the news the sponsors had agreed to accept the equivalent of $90,000 for their investment, to be paid in a nine year period at the rate of $10,000 each year.

Governor Bradford and seven other men agreed to assume responsibility for the payments, and the other citizens would pay either three bushels of corn for each family member or six pounds of tobacco.

In 1629 and 1630, the last members of the Leyden worshippers arrived. William Bradford had made allotments of land to each family so they could grow their own food in 1623, and these new arrivals meant more land would have to be allotted. Moreover, the current citizens had to provide the new arrivals with shelter and food until they could manage on their own, and further aggravating the colonists, a larger amount would be owed to their English sponsors — in fact, the equivalent of $27,500 more, according to Allerton.

When Plymouth citizens complained about the increasing debt burden, the Undertakers told them they would assume all the debt, which would prove disastrous to some in later years, as they would have to sell their property to pay it.

Everyone who emigrated to New England did not share the religious beliefs and practices of the Pilgrims. In 1625, a colony called Mount Wollaston (after the Captain who founded it) had been started 25 miles north of Plymouth.

Thomas Morton, Alice Bradford's sister's nephew, was a partner of Captain Wollaston, who had arrived in New England with the hope of making great riches in the area.

The accumulation of riches would require labor, so Captain Wollaston sold some of the colonists who had come from England with him into slavery!

Thomas Morton told the men still at Mount Wollaston what had happened, and he promised that if they would stay with him, he would share equally with them in any profits they made in trading ventures.

Until this time, Plymouth officials had ignored the new colony and did not perceive it to be a threat. A short time after Morton took control, it became obvious that Wollaston colonists were not God-fearing citizens seeking religious freedom. They had wild parties to celebrate their new name of "Ma-re Mount" (Latin for "Mountain by the Sea") and to commemorate any other event anyone could think of to give them an excuse for revelry and debauchery.

An 80 foot Maypole was erected in the middle of the village, around which Morton, his men and friendly Indian women danced, singing and laughing loudly, having spent the previous hours drinking wine and beer.

Governor Bradford and other Plymouth leaders dubbed the neighboring colony "Merry Mount," believing it more fitting. It was when the Plymouth citizens began to meet with greater frequency Indians armed with guns that they felt the operations at Merry Mount must be stopped.

Captain Miles Standish was sent by Governor Bradford to take control of Merry Mount. Standish and his men found the Merry Mount colonists so drunk they could neither aim nor shoot their guns to defend themselves, so Standish and his group easily captured them and took them to Plymouth.

Morton was sent back to England, but he had his final revenge when he wrote *New England Canaan*, a satiric account of the pilgrims and their lives.

Alice Bradford was literate, one of the few educated women in Plymouth, having attended school in either England or Holland. When Doctor Samuel Fuller's wife, Bridget, started a "dame school" in Plymouth in 1635, William Bradford, Jr., and his brother, Joseph, were among Dame Fuller's students. In keeping with custom, Mercy Bradford probably remained at home with her mother to learn housekeeping skills, but Alice may have also taught her daughter to read and write.

Isaac Allerton was sent back to England to secure an official patent of the Plymouth settlement. They wanted boundaries extended to include the trading post they had established earlier.

Allerton returned with a patent without the Great Seal affixed, which made it worthless, and he brought Thomas Morton back with him as his secretary. Given Morton's past, Plymouth officials began to investigate Allerton's actions on their behalf, as they had noticed their debt never seemed to get smaller. They found Allerton had been buying merchandise in England to establish his own trading post and had charged it to Plymouth's account.

It was natural that all these questionable actions by Allerton would lead to dissension between William Brewster and the other Undertakers. He defended his son-in-law's honesty, and because of the great respect the Undertakers had for Brewster, they dropped their charges about Allerton.

Allerton continued to abuse the trust placed in him, however, and by the time the complicated financial deals had been analyzed, the Undertakers found their debt had increased from $20,000 to $238,500 (modern equivalents) in the past four years!

To satisfy financial claims against them, William Bradford sold much of his acreage, as did both John Alden and Miles Standish.

Alice and William Bradford watched sadly as their old friends and neighbors began moving to other locations. Some Plymouth citizens established a new colony called Marshfield which became the home of the Edward Winslow family. John and Priscilla Alden had moved earlier to Duxbury, and John Bradford and his wife, the former Martha Bourne, whom he married in 1640, joined the Aldens there in 1645. They never had any children. They moved on to Marshfield in 1653, then to Norwich, Connecticut, in 1660. John Bradford died there in 1678.

William Bradford, now the only original leader of Plymouth who had remained in the colony, continued to grieve about the decline of both Plymouth village and the church. He had begun writing his history of the Plymouth colony in his journal entitled "Of Plymouth Plantation" in 1630. His chronicle of events ended in 1650 when he noted that Edward Winslow "was detained [in England] longer than was expected, and afterward fell into other employments there, so as he hath been absent this four years, which hath been much to the weakening of this government, without whose consent he took these employments upon him."

William Bradford died early in May 1657, having continued to govern until his death. He left an estate of more than three hundred acres of land along the Jones River, a house with an orchard and gardens in Plymouth, a library of more than three hundred volumes, various pieces of silver and pewter, as well as clothing. According to a 1985 calculation, Bradford's estate was worth the equivalent of $75,000.

In 1646, Alice Bradford's sister Mary Carpenter had come to live with Alice and William. She had never married and was living alone in England. She remained with Alice the rest of her life, dying in Plymouth in 1667.

Alice Bradford's oldest son, Constant Southworth, married Elizabeth Collier in 1637, and they had eight children. Constant served as treasurer of Plymouth from 1659 until his death 20 years later.

Thomas Southworth married Elizabeth Reyner in 1637 and worked at the Kennebec River Trading Post from 1651 to 1654 as a representative of his stepfather's interests there. Thomas also served as assistant governor of Plymouth and as a commissioner of the New England Confederacy until his death in 1669. He and his wife had one child.

William Bradford, Jr., was married twice and had a total of 15 children. As a major in King Philip's War, he commanded two companies of Plymouth soldiers and was seriously wounded in the Great Swamp massacre. He died around 1692. He inherited his father's "Of Plymouth Plantation" as well as other property.

Mercy Bradford was named a beneficiary in her father's will, as was her brother Joseph, but few other details are available about them.

Alice Bradford survived her husband by 13 years, dying in 1670 at 80 years of age. She was also named in Bradford's will, which referred to her as "a blessed mother in Israel."

A monument was erected in Alice's memory on Burial Hill in Plymouth. Alice's epitaph calls her a "godly matron."

Bibliography

Bradford, William. *Of Plymouth Plantation: The Pilgrims In America.* Edited by Harvey Wish. New York: Capricorn Books, 1962.

Gill, Crispin. *Mayflower Remembered: A History of the Plymouth Pilgrims.* New York: Taplinger, 1970.

Haller, William. *The Rise of Puritanism.* New York: Columbia University Press, 1938.

Willison, George F. *Saints and Strangers.* New York: TIME, 1964.

3

Margaret Tyndal Winthrop

When she married John Winthrop in April 1618, Margaret Tyndal was age 27, older than most women marrying for the first time. John had been a widower for the past 15 months, since the death of his second wife.

Margaret's family's home in Great Maplestead in Essex was called Chelmsley House. It was a fine manor house that her father, Sir John Tyndal, had built for his family.

Sir John was a master in Chancery and had been murdered two years earlier by a Mr. Bertram when he ruled against Bertram in a trial involving damages of less than £200.

Lady Anne Egerton Tyndal encouraged her daughter to marry John Winthrop, whom she considered to be a fine man, even if he had adopted the strong belief that the Anglican Church needed to be purified from within. Margaret held the same view, and they were considered a good match when they wed in a brick church in Great Maplestead.

John Winthrop's first wife, Mary Forth Winthrop, had not been a religious zealot. She listened to her husband's religious ideas and did not oppose him in any way, but she never became as enthusiastic about reforming the Anglican Church.

Mary and John had had six children before her death in 1615. His second marriage to Thomasine Clopton occurred six months later, but both Thomasine and their newborn daughter died the next year.

Shortly after John married Margaret, he assumed the care and control of Groton Manor, his family's estate. Margaret brought a substantial dowry to the marriage, as had John's previous wives. Whatever future problems the newlyweds might encounter, they would be well off financially.

Groton Manor had been part of a monastery in Suffolk before the Reformation, and when the monastery property was confiscated by King Henry VIII of England in 1544, John Winthrop's grandfather bought the country estate.

When they reached the manor after their wedding, John's children, John, Jr., Henry, Forth and Mary, welcomed Margaret warmly, especially John, Jr., who was fond of his stepmother from the first moment he saw her. Later in life he declared Margaret was "as deare to my selfe" as his own mother had been. Adam Winthrop II, John's father, and Adam's wife, Anne Bowne, and their daughter, Lucy, were also members of the household, and they were enthusiastic about Margaret's joining their group.

Margaret's new home was a lovely estate containing more than 500 acres of rolling hills, fields filled with various grain crops, patches of woodland to be used for fuel and hunting, and scattered farm ponds stocked with fish. There were barns for both cattle and horses, including fine saddle horses. Tenants on the estate cared for the large flocks of sheep kept by the Winthrops.

There were at least nine servants to do housework. The duties in such households were numerous and laborious:

> Mondays — Look out the foul clothes, and call the maids and sit or stay by them till they be all mended.
> Tuesdays — Clean the rooms and chairs from the Great Room to the nursery, and the beds on top and bottom, and dust the feathers.
> Wednesday — Clean all the rooms' chairs and beds

under and top with the feathers (dusters) from the nursery to the aisle chamber.

Thursday — Clean the hall and parlor's windows, tables, chairs and pictures below-stairs.

Friday — Scour all the grates, tongs and irons.

Saturday — Clean the storehouse, shelves and dressers.

Every day — Once for one hour in the forenoon go through all the rooms and see it does not rain into them and dust them all down and swipe them.

Dairy-maid — Wash your dairy every day and for your milk and butter do as you will be directed. Churn Tuesdays and Fridays. Serve the swine and poultry night and morning, and for the hogs-meat any of the servant men shall carry that out for you. Observe well the time for setting all sorts of your poultry, once every week make your house bread and the same shall help you knead it.

Cook-maid — Wash your kitchen every night and the larders every other day, shelves and dressers, and scour the pewter we use every Friday night and all the rest of the pewter once every month. Keep your kitchen extra-ordinary clean. To help on washing days the rest of the maids wash. And make all the maids bring down their candlesticks the first thing in the morning to be made clean.

These directions were for the servants in a manor in Suffolk not far from Groton Manor, but all households were operated on basically the same schedule.

Margaret and John lived contented lives at Groton Manor, and their first child, a son named Stephen, was born the next year. Two more sons, Adam and Dean, soon followed. A daughter born in 1625 died in infancy, and their fourth son, Samuel, was born in 1627.

At the time of their marriage, John was employed as a drafts-man of bills in Parliament. He continued in this job until 1629, when King Charles I dissolved the Parliament. The King indicated he had no intention of calling Parliament into session again any time soon. He would be in complete control of the government.

John Winthrop found himself unemployed at a time when prices rose each month due to the war England was fighting with Spain. Even though he received an income from Groton Manor, it had never been sufficient to support the needs of his family because the expenses of maintaining the estate were so great.

John had heard of a group of English investors who were recruiting people to go to the New World. The investors planned to establish a new colony there and buy furs from the native Indians. Now in its fifteenth year, the English colony at Plymouth was still struggling to survive. In fact, John Winthrop, Jr., had mentioned the latest project to his father a year earlier and wanted to travel ahead with an advance party.

The more John Winthrop considered the new Massachusetts Bay Company colonization project, the more he liked it. His son Henry had gone to Barbados two years before, but had not been successful in his financial dealings there. Henry was presently back in England, living a drunken, dissipated life, and his father was deeply concerned about him.

John came to a decision. If Margaret agreed, they would all go to live in the Massachusetts Bay Colony. In England, John suffered many temptations that might be easier to control in a simpler environment. John, Jr., had already shown his willingness to emigrate, and poor, confused Henry could be led away from his present sinful life if he was not with his disreputable friends, or so his father reasoned.

Margaret assured John she was willing to go with him to New England, and they began making arrangements to leave. John and two of his sons would go first and get houses built for each of their families, and the women and younger people could follow later. Groton Manor would be sold to provide money for the venture.

Young John and his wife Martha would stay in England to help

Margaret sell the estate and take care of her during her impending sixth childbirth. Henry's wife was also pregnant, and both women preferred to stay in England until the babies were born.

In a letter she wrote to him while he was in London on business in the autumn of 1629, Margaret indicated her willingness to accompany her husband:

> My dear husband ... I know not how to express my love to thee or my desires of thy wished welfare, but my heart is well known to thee.... My thoughts are now on our great change and alteration of our course here, which I beseech the Lord to bless us in. If the Lord be with us who can be against us: my grief is the fear of staying behind thee, but I must leave all to the good providence of God.... Your faithful wife, Margaret Winthrop

John's reply to her, dated November 12, 1629, showed his deep affection for her, and her acceptance of his decision to take his family away from England was welcome:

> My sweet wife, I received thy most kind letter.... And blessed by God who hath given me a wife, who is such a help and encouragement to me in this great work, wherein so many wives are so great a hindrance to theirs. I doubt not but the Lord will recompense abundantly the faithfulness of thy love and obedience....

The members of the Massachusetts Bay Colony were delighted to have prospective colonists of the caliber and ability of the Winthrops join their group. As preparations continued for their departure, John found himself appointed the acting director of the venture!

Later, on October 20, 1629, he was officially elected the governor by the General Court of the company, almost a year before he and the others would leave England.

John's elevation to governor proved a mixed blessing, however, as he now had to assume responsibility for making all the arrangements for ships to carry the prospective colonists and their possessions, as well as stock provisions for their journey. He spent little time at Groton Manor during this hectic, busy time.

One of John's concerns, shared by other Puritan believers who would be traveling with him, was the charge that they were running away from the present problems in the Anglican Church. John and other members of the group published a statement in which they avowed their love for the Anglican Church and declared they had no wish or plans to separate themselves from the Church of England, as the Puritan colonists at Plymouth had done. The colonists at Plymouth were called Separatists, and Winthrop did not want to be considered one of their group.

On March 28, 1630, John and a number of other people boarded the ship *Arbella*. John wrote Margaret:

> And now my sweet soul, I must once again take my last farewell of thee in old England. It goeth very near to my heart to leave thee. ... I hope the cause we have agreed upon will be some ease to us both. On Mondays and Fridays, at five of the clock at night, we shall meet in spirit till we meet in person.... Therefore, I will only take thee now and my sweet children in mine arms, and kiss and embrace you all.... Thine wheresoever,
>
> John Winthrop

John was on board the flagship of the expedition, which had four ships in the group, when they sailed on April 8, 1630. Four hundred passengers went on the voyage, all hoping to find a better life in Massachusetts Bay.

When they finally arrived in the Salem area of Massachusetts, the new arrivals found poor living conditions of only rude huts for shelter, made with mud-daubed walls and reed thatched roofs.

Henry drowned on July 2, 1630, only three days after his arrival, when he stepped into a tidal creek. His survivors were a wife and little daughter.

John wrote a letter to Margaret on July 30, 1630, from his new location in the Charlestowne area:

> My dear wife ... now (my good wife) let us join in praising our merciful God, that howsoever he hath afflicted us, both generally and particularly my own family in his stroke upon my son Henry, yet myself and the rest of our children and family are safe and in good health. And our fare be but coarse in respect to what we formerly had, (pease, puddings and fish being our ordinary diet) yet he makes it sweet and wholesome to us, that I may truly say I desire no better.... I see no cause to repent of our coming thither. Thy faithful husband,
>
> J. W.

Back in England, Margaret and John, Jr., were encountering numerous problems in selling Groton Manor. Farming had become unprofitable as grain had lost a fourth of its value, and wool was selling for a much lower price than at the time John left. They did sell the property at last, but only received 75 percent of the amount John had hoped to get.

While waiting to join her husband, Margaret gave birth to a daughter, whom she named Anne.

In Massachusetts, John had moved from Charlestowne on to another location to found the "city on the hill" he had envisioned during the sea voyage. The supply of water at Salem had been insufficient to support a colony of the size he planned. In the latest location he believed it would be completely satisfactory, and the colonists began their work of building houses for their families. The colony would become the city of Boston.

A severe epidemic struck the new settlement shortly after their arrival, possibly from either the water they drank or from seafood they ate. Adding to their misery, on the day before Christmas, a winter storm struck with high winds and blizzard-like conditions.

Winthrop saw eleven of the servants he had brought with him sicken and die, despite his efforts to save them. He never became ill, although his sons, Adam and Stephen, did. Each eventually recovered.

John retained his enthusiasm for the venture despite the hardships, and wrote Margaret:

> I thank God, I like so well to be here, as I do not repent my coming and if I were to come again, I would not have altered my course, though I had foreseen all these afflictions. I never fared better in my life, never slept better, never had more content of mind.

Many colonists suffered in Boston that winter despite John's firm belief in the ultimate success of the colony. The severe cold weather caused more colonists to develop pneumonia and other respiratory illnesses, which led to more deaths. In an effort to keep warm, some of the colonists built fires too large in their hastily constructed fireplaces (with chimneys made of mud-coated wood), and their straw-thatched roofs caught fire.

Two hundred people died that winter. John worked hard to encourage his fellow colonists to continue living in the settlement.

Winthrop had built a house for his family in Boston, and he also acquired six hundred acres of land lying along the Mystic River. On this latter property he had a stone house built. He complained that wolves were a constant threat, and he always carried a gun when he went to the farm.

Conditions continued to worsen in Boston to such an extent that eighty of the surviving colonists returned to England as soon as they could get passage on a ship. When they told their England sponsors about their difficulties in Massachusetts, the sponsors began to fear they would not even recoup their original investment.

John Winthrop bought food and other needed supplies for the remaining colonists with his own money. He did not want Margaret and his other children to suffer as he, Adam and Stephen had, so he wrote Margaret, sending a detailed list of supplies he wanted her to bring. He told her he wanted his family

> to be warm clothed and have a store of fresh provisions, meal, eggs put up in salt or ground malt, butter, oatmeal, peas and fruit, and a large strong chest or two, well-locked, to keep these provisions in.... Be sure to have ready at sea two or three skillets of several sizes, a large frying pan, and a case to boil a pudding in, a store of linen for use at sea ... some drinking vessels and pewter and other vessels.... Remember to come well furnished with linen, woolen, some more bedding, brass, pewter, leather bottles, drinking horns, etc.... Let my son provide twelve axes of several sorts ... whatever they cost, and some augers, great and small ... (and) candles, soap and a store of beef suet....

The house John built for Margaret was large by colony standards. It was constructed of rough sawn boards, had a reed-thatched roof and the usual wooden chimney lined inside with dried clay mud. The three rooms on the first floor were the kitchen, main hall and a bedroom with beds and chests. The main hall was used as a living room. Two more bedrooms and a study were on the second floor.

Margaret finally reached Boston on November 4, 1631, aboard the ship *Lyon*. The trip had been long and harrowing, and was marred tragically by the death of the Winthrops' baby daughter, Anne. John never saw the child, who was buried at sea.

John Winthrop, Jr., and his wife Martha, his sister Mary and Henry's widow and baby daughter came with Margaret. Dean Winthrop was nine years old, and he stayed in England to continue his education.

Poor Margaret! Even though she was reunited with her beloved

husband, she must have suffered a shock when she surveyed the primitive living conditions in the colony. She still grieved about her baby's
death at sea, their house was extremely scanty compared to Groton
Manor, and even the food was different.

Margaret learned that bread in their New World was made from
cracked or ground corn instead of the barley or wheat used in England. Squashes and pumpkins grew in abundance, but none of the
Winthrops had ever eaten them before. Fish and other seafood were
different, and all the berries and some fruits were new to them.

She had servants to help her with household chores, but there
were few utensils with which to work. She supervised all tasks to
make sure they were done well.

Religious meetings took several hours of her time each week,
and there were letters to write and visitors to entertain.

Margaret and John were happy to be living together again, and
as time passed they hoped life would be as pleasant as it had been in
England.

Margaret gave birth to a son named William in August 1632, but
he died in infancy, as did the little daughter named Sarah born in 1634.

Margaret was a good-natured woman and friendly by all accounts
written about her. She was glad when new neighbors moved in across
the street from Winthrop home in November 1634. They were
William and Anne Hutchinson and their children.

Anne Hutchinson was an experienced midwife. If Margaret
needed her, Anne was there, and the two women became good friends.
Anne had lost several children, and she could sympathize with Margaret. Both women were 43 years old and both were from similar
middle-class backgrounds. Furthermore, both women were literate,
which was not common among the first women colonists, and both
were deeply religious, each basing her life on religious teachings.

In their attitudes about women's rights and abilities, however,
Margaret and Anne were poles apart. Margaret was a "silent, subordinate helpmate," to quote John Winthrop, while Anne felt she had

a right to speak out and argue with men about issues that concerned her. William Hutchinson supported his wife in her beliefs about equality among the sexes.

John Winthrop was now in firm control of the governmental affairs in Boston, even if other men held the title of governor from time to time. Winthrop had saved the colony during its early days, and his influence was pervasive throughout colonial and church affairs.

William Hutchinson was a businessman who sold textiles. He had come to Massachusetts in an attempt to earn more money and to escape the many rules and regulations imposed on businesses in England.

The Puritan preacher now serving the Boston Church was well known to the Hutchinsons before they came to Boston. The Reverend John Cotton had held services near their English home for several years before coming to Massachusetts.

Anne Hutchinson was so impressed by Mr. Cotton's religious beliefs and teachings that she began holding meetings for women in her home in England, where they discussed and reviewed the Reverend Cotton's sermons. Anne was the daughter of an Anglican minister and was well-informed on Bible teachings.

With their move to the Boston area, Anne saw no reason not to begin holding the same type of meetings for women in the colony. At first, there were few objections. The women were hungry for companionship, and they had few contacts with other women except at church. They flocked to Anne's house, where they discussed religion, their children, childbirth, household problems and other subjects of interest to them. Margaret Winthrop joined the group.

When William Hutchinson saw how well received his wife's meetings were, he began holding similar gatherings for his fellow businessmen. That was when the Hutchinsons' activities began to attract official notice in Boston.

In addition to discussing religion, the men began exploring ways they could prevent the imposition of wage and price controls on their businesses, as voted by the ruling council of Boston.

John Winthrop was firmly convinced these controls were essential, but the businessmen had come to Massachusetts to escape the rigid control that the English government exerted over their lives. They did not want the same sort of regulations in Boston.

Winthrop knew if he began an open conflict with men in the colony, many of them would either move on elsewhere to operate their businesses or return to England. He knew Boston needed traders of all kinds to prosper and become a viable city.

That was a possible explanation for Winthrop's extreme dislike of Anne and her meetings. If Anne could be silenced and banished, William would leave also.

Anne Hutchinson was called into Boston's General Court to answer charges that she showed disrespect for colonial authority. Margaret Winthrop was confused by the hostility her husband evinced for Anne. Anne had been a valued confidante for Margaret when she sorely needed a friend.

When John was away on a business trip during these troubled days, Margaret wrote him:

Sad Boston, 1637

Dear, in my thoughts I blush to think how much I have neglected the opportunity of presenting my love to you. Sad thoughts possess my spirits, and I cannot repulse them, which makes me unfit for anything, wondering what the Lord means by all these troubles among us. Sure as I am, that all shall work to the best to them that love God, or rather are loved of him. I know He will bring light out of obscurity and make his righteousness shine forth as clear as the noon day. Yet I find myself an adverse spirit, and a trembling heart, not so willing to submit to the will of God as I desire. There is a time to plant and a time to pull up that which is planted, which I could desire might not be yet....

Your loving wife, Margaret

Clearly Margaret had no wish to antagonize her husband by questioning his reasons for his campaign against Anne and her beliefs, but, just as clearly, she did not want her good friend to move away from Boston.

John Winthrop continued stubbornly to press for Anne's banishment from the colony. When he attained his goal at last in March 1638, the banishment included the entire Hutchinson family, including Anne's sister's family and all supporters of Anne's religious views.

Young John Winthrop did not oppose his father openly about his vindictive treatment of Mrs. Hutchinson, but it is noteworthy that the younger Winthrop did not attend any meetings of Boston colony officials during this period of time, even though he was a member of that body. A short time later he moved his family away from the Boston area and went to live in Connecticut permanently.

Anne Hutchinson did not want to leave Boston and had hoped either Margaret Winthrop or John Cotton's wife, Sarah, another good friend, might come forward to speak on her behalf, but they were silent.

When Anne suffered a miscarriage of her pregnancy as a result of the long hours she was forced to stand in the cold courtroom during her trial, Margaret must have felt the punishment was greater than the offense, since she knew how keen the grief could be from the loss of a child. Nevertheless, she did not question John openly.

Margaret Winthrop never saw her friend Anne again. The Hutchinson family went to live in the colony of Rhode Island, which had been started by another religious dissident named Roger Williams.

Margaret had no more children, and she died (probably of influenza) ten years later at age 56 on June 14, 1647. Her grave is reportedly located beside that of her husband in King's Chapel Churchyard in Boston.

John Winthrop remarried six months after Margaret's death and fathered another son before his own death on March 26, 1649.

Margaret's first-born son, Stephen, had returned to England to live some years earlier. He wrote his brother John, Jr., in 1650 concerning their father's intolerance of religious beliefs differing from his own:

> God declares ... particularly against that spirit.... The Lord in mercy keep it from ... (your settlement) or else it will spoil your farmers, ship and iron works.

John Winthrop, Jr., was elected governor of Connecticut in 1657 and never lived in Boston again.

Bibliography

Black, Robert C. III. *The Younger John Winthrop.* New York: Columbia University Press, 1966.

Earle, Alice Morse. *Margaret Winthrop.* New York: Scribners', 1895.

Hanscom, Elizabeth Deering, ed. *The Heart of the Puritan: Selections from Letters and Journals.* New York: Macmillan, 1917.

Morgan, Edmund S. *The Puritan Dilemma: The Story of John Winthrop.* Boston: Little, Brown, 1958.

4

Margaret Brent

Lord Baltimore II was the holder of a patent granted by King
Charles I for the settlement of the Maryland area of the New World
of America. In the autumn of 1633, Lord Baltimore spent a large part
of his fortune outfitting two ships, the *Ark* and the *Dove*, to carry
colonists to the proposed colony. The venture was in the care and
control of Leonard Calvert, Lord Baltimore's brother.

The Calverts were Catholics, and they urged fellow believers in
England to emigrate to their colony, but since there were not enough
Catholics interested in the project, many of the first arrivals were
Protestants. The colony, in fact, never became predominantly Catholic.

Lord Baltimore did not expect his settlers to engage in fur trading as had the financiers of the Plymouth and Massachusetts Bay
colonies. Lord Baltimore planned to recover his investment by granting tracts of land to the colonists, on which the recipients would
always have to pay rent. The quitrent on the property was paid faithfully by the settlers until the time of the American Revolution.

The Calverts promised religious freedom to any and all persons
who went to Maryland, and they actively encouraged women to
become colonists by agreeing to make land grants to them in their
own names. Women of any age could receive 100 acres at first; later,
this was reduced to 50 acres each to women between 14 and 40 years
of age.

In 1634 Leonard Calvert and three Jesuit priests selected a likely site for a colony at the mouth of the Potomac River. The colony, named St. Mary's, was more peaceful and cohesive than other colonies nearby, even as it grew. There was never a "starving time" such as the Pilgrims had suffered in the Massachusetts colonies, and the Indians living nearby were friendly and few in numbers.

Margaret and Mary Brent, sisters and the daughters of Richard and Elizabeth Reed Brent of Gloucester, England, came to Maryland on November 22, 1638, along with their two brothers, Giles and Fulke. They were accompanied by nine other settlers.

Margaret was about 37 years old when she arrived in Maryland, and Mary was younger. They received land grants of 70½ acres and decided to stay in the Saint Mary's City area, the capital of the Maryland colony. Each woman had brought servants with her, each had manor houses built, and each started her own plantation, as did Giles Brent. Fulke returned to England in spring 1639.

In time Margaret controlled more than 1,000 acres of Maryland land. All the Brents were familiar with the management of plantations, as their Catholic father was a wealthy landowner in England.

Soon the colony's court-baron and court-leet sessions were held in Mary's home, named Saint Gabriel's Manor, on Kent Island. Margaret's home was known as Resurrection Manor.

Father Andrew White, a Catholic priest, accompanied the first colonists to Maryland, but he devoted much of his time and attention to converting the nearby Indians to Christianity.

Captain Thomas Cornwallis brought so many servants with him that he was entitled to receive 2,000 acres of land. An Anglican minister, Reverend Robert Brooke, received 4,100 acres.

The large land tracts were known as manors, and the owners or lords of the manors were judges of their servants' and tenants' disputes, and could punish them for minor infractions of the law.

Margaret Brent was a truly outstanding business woman. She and her relatives had come to Maryland primarily to escape the religious persecution by the Church of England, whose members had hated Catholics since the Reformation.

When Governor Leonard Calvert returned to England in 1643 to consult with Lord Baltimore about the colony's affairs, some rebels, Puritan in belief and led by William Claiborne of the Kent Island colony and settler Richard Ingle, tried to incite their followers to stage a coup and overthrow the government of the colony.

Giles Brent was acting governor of Maryland in Calvert's absence. In an excess of Puritan zeal, the band of rebels condemned ten people to death, hanged four, took property belonging to some of the colonists and drove out the priests, who fled to Virginia.

Richard Ingle took Giles Brent to England as his prisoner after the rebellion. When Governor Calvert returned from England, he also had to seek refuge in Virginia, along with some of the other officials in his government.

Margaret Brent owned property on Kent Island, having acquired 1,000 acres from her brother Giles to settle debts he owed her and other family members. There were several houses on the land, which were occupied by families who raised tobacco crops and tended livestock for her.

During the Claiborne-led coup, the Brents' property was taken, but Margaret and Mary continued to buy and sell property and conduct business for their brothers, and Margaret signed documents as "Attorney for my brother."

The Brents may have been related to Governor Calvert and Lord Baltimore. If true, that would explain why Calvert and Margaret were joint guardians of Mary Kitomaquund, the daughter of the Piscataway Indian chief. The chief had entrusted his daughter to the settlers in order for her to receive an education.

Margaret pursued her debtors with such fervor that court records of the province show her name appearing 124 times in the years 1642 to 1650, the majority of the cases being decided in her favor.

In 1645 Governor Calvert's supporters regained control of the

Maryland colony, and order was restored. Margaret recovered the property she owned on Kent Island, even though William Claiborne, who had a trading post on the island, claimed it constituted an established colony and that he had a prior claim. Margaret had Kent Island declared a county, and delegates were sent to represent them at Assembly meetings.

To the dismay of his relatives, friends and fellow Catholics, Governor Calvert died unexpectedly on June 9, 1646. Just before his death he named Thomas Greene to be the new governor, and he named Margaret to be the sole executrix of his estate. Margaret was told to "take all and pay all."

Giles Brent was returning to Maryland from England when Governor Calvert died, and he might have been named executor if he had been present.

Margaret went to work collecting money due Calvert's estate and settling law suits against the estate by his creditors. She faced a major dilemma when the captain of the militia at Fort Inigoes demanded pay for his soldiers. His men had come from Virginia, fought loyally to regain control of Maryland for Governor Calvert and had succeeded. The governor had pledged they would be paid if it took his entire estate.

Governor Calvert's estate, however, was not worth enough to provide pay for the soldiers. In fact, his estate consisted of "an old bed and bolster with an old green rug for a coverlet, a very old featherbed, a flock bed, bolster and old red rug; an old trunk with lock and key, a small trunk and white box; a square chest, a 'joined table and two chairs', an old chair frame and a rug."

He also left a blue jug, five old pewter dishes, a basin, five plates, twelve pewter spoons, a silver sack cup and three small bits of silverplate. His kitchen utensils consisted of an iron pot and an old brass kettle.

Margaret faced the most serious financial problem of her life. As days passed, the soldiers became hungry, and they threatened to stage a rebellion of their own against the present government if they were not paid.

  Margaret knew she must act, so she sold cattle belonging to the colonists in common to get money. She bought corn from the Virginia colony to feed the soldiers and paid their wages from the money she had received from the cattle sale. The men were satisfied, and trouble was averted by her courageous actions.

When Lord Baltimore in London learned that Margaret had sold proprietary cattle to obtain funds to operate the colonial government business, he complained to the Assembly that she had usurped authority to act for the colony, and he demanded she be reprimanded for her actions!

The Assembly, however, defended Margaret's actions in a letter to Lord Baltimore: "as for Mrs. Brent's undertaking and meddling with your Lordship's estate here ... we do verily believe and in conscience report that it was better for colony's safety at that time in her hands than in any man's else in the province. She rather deserved favor and thanks from your Honor for her so much concurring to the public safety than to be liable to all those bitter invectives you have been pleased to express against her."

In London, Puritans had gained control of Parliament, and Lord Baltimore feared they would take his proprietorship away from him. He turned against his Catholic friends and supporters and began granting concessions to Protestants.

In August 1648, Lord Baltimore replaced Governor Greene, a Catholic, with a man named William Stone, a Protestant. In 1649 a Toleration Act was passed by the Assembly legislators, which recognized the right to freedom of religious worship for all settlers. The act imposed penalties on those who used nicknames or made pointed derogatory remarks about any person's religion or its practices.

On January 21, 1648, Maryland Assembly Records show: "Came Mrs. Margaret Brent and requested to have vote in the House for herself and voyce [voice] also, for that on the last Court third January, it was ordered that the said Mrs. Brent was to be looked upon and received as his Lordship's attorney. The Governor denied that the said Mrs. Brent should have any vote in the house. And the said Mrs. Brent protested against all proceedings in this present Assembly she may be present and have vote as aforesaid."

Governor Stone provided a refuge for a persecuted Puritan group of colonists living in Virginia, and he added Protestant members to the Ruling Assembly.

Giles Brent married the Indian girl Mary Kitomaquund, and Lord Baltimore feared Giles hoped to gain more land and power by reason of his marriage.

In 1651 Margaret was accused of killing cattle living in the wild and selling the beef. She insisted the cattle were her own, and she asked for a jury trial, during which she was acquitted.

Giles Brent moved to Virginia in 1650, and Margaret and Mary followed him after Margaret's trial. They established a plantation they named "Peace" in Westmoreland County. The Toleration Act was repealed by the Maryland provincial government the next year, and they now forbade Catholic believers to attend Mass, confession or show any other manifestation of their religion. It was well the Brents had moved to Virginia.

In 1658 Margaret Brent reappeared in Maryland courts to press her claim as heir to an estate left to her as a token of love and affection by a suitor. There is no other record of Margaret's activities in courts after that date.

Margaret Brent died sometime before 1671, as her will was probated in May of that year. She gave away her extensive rights to land in Maryland in her will.

Margaret Brent's niece and namesake married George Plowden, son of Sir Edmund Plowden, Earl of Albion, England, and the newlyweds lived in Resurrection Manor after their wedding and for years after. Their descendants live in Maryland today.

Bibliography

Brugger, Robert J. *Maryland: A Middle Temperament.* Baltimore: Johns Hopkins University Press, 1980.

Chapelle, Suzanne E. Greene, et al. *Maryland: A History of Its People.* Baltimore: Johns Hopkins University Press, 1973.

Wilstach, Paul. *Tidewater Maryland.* Indianapolis: Bobbs-Merrill, 1931.

5

Anne Marbury Hutchinson

Anne Hutchinson proved that some of the Puritans did not come to the New World seeking religious freedom for all people, but only for themselves. To disagree with Governor John Winthrop and his associates about religious matters was forbidden, and such disagreement led to Anne's banishment from the Massachusetts Bay Colony.

Anne was born in Alford in Lincolnshire, England, on July 17, 1591, the second daughter of Francis and Bridget Dryden Marbury. Alford was a small country village, but the Marbury family was important among the citizens.

Francis Marbury had been a schoolmaster of the Alford School for ten years preceding Anne's birth, and had also been a preacher at the church of Saint Wilfrid, which was 250 years old. About the time of Anne's birth, Mr. Marbury lost both his teaching job and his license to preach because of some of the religious views he held.

For the next three years, he was forced to live a life of idleness in regard to employment, and baby Anne had his undivided care and attention. He regained his license some time later, but he continued to instruct Anne. He taught her not only about religious matters, but also drama, politics and literature. Anne was an eager student, and she listened in rapt silence as her father described the persecution to which he had been subjected because he had criticized some of the religious practices of the Church of England.

When Queen Elizabeth I died, King James I came to the English throne, and this led indirectly to a change for the better in the fortunes of the Marbury family.

When Anne was fourteen, her father was appointed to be the pastor of a prestigious London church, Saint Martin's, and the Marburys moved in 1605 from their country home in Alford to London.

Anne found living in London to be different from simple country life. She enjoyed living in the warmer London house, which was heated with coal instead of wood. There were new foods to eat, especially imported ones, such as oranges, peaches and figs. The Thames River, with its flocks of majestic white swans swimming up and down, also held her attention. The biggest difference she found though was all the bustling activity in London.

One feature of their new location Anne did not like was the stifling smell of raw sewage running in large open ditches along the city streets. This was the only system the city had for the disposal of sewage, and rainfall or street sweepers got rid of it once a week, theoretically. In the country the Marburys had emptied their chamberpots some distance from the house, and there was no odor.

Anne liked the glass windows in many of the London houses. The cost of glass was beyond the income of Alford residents, and no one there had such luxury in their homes.

As he aged, Mr. Marbury mellowed somewhat in his attitudes toward the officials of the Anglican Church, but he still believed there was much about the church that needed changing. He felt more free to express his views in London since there was less danger of retribution (King James was more anti–Catholic than pro–Church of England). Also Mr. Marbury's parishioners in London were chiefly wine merchants who worried more about how they would pay their taxes than about the theological beliefs of their pastor.

As Anne matured, she assisted her mother during the births of her younger brothers and sisters, and as a result Anne developed an interest in midwifery. She retained this interest for the rest of her life and endeavored to improve her skills. She also noted the herbal remedies used by her mother and neighbors when they treated sick family members.

Anne could never hope to get a medical education, as no medical college of that time would accept a woman as a student. All her brothers would eventually graduate from Oxford University, even though Mr. Marbury died in 1611. Anne's education, on the other hand, consisted of learning to run a household and the care for children.

Women in England, as well as many of the men, had a desire to "purify" the Anglican Church, and they spoke openly about the need for reform, especially in London. Anne went to hear some of the women speak.

Church officials resented the efforts of the reformers, however, and many of them were forced to leave England to escape persecution. It was during this period that the Pilgrims who later settled Plymouth went to live in Leyden, Holland. Their difficulties reminded Anne of the problems her father had endured in his life, and their misfortunes made a profound impression on her.

On August 9, 1612, Anne Marbury married William Hutchinson, also a native of Alford. The young couple had known each other since childhood. Now in his middle twenties, young William had become a prosperous sheep farmer and textile dealer. Anne was 21 at the time of her marriage.

The newlyweds settled down in their own home in Alford, located near the home of William's parents. The home was much above average for the time, having ten rooms, including a study and a pantry. It was furnished with massive oak furniture, pegged, rather than nailed, at the jointures. They had canopied beds and even a wooden bathing tub.

The house was wooden-frame construction with the walls made of woven straw, liberally daubed with clay mud, and it had a roof made of thatched straw. They owned some pieces of silver and pewter table furnishings, such as spoons and candlesticks. They had the usual long-handled iron and brass cooking utensils.

Their first child, a son named Edward, was born a year later, and the young Hutchinsons had many friends in the community to welcome him, as both Anne and William were personable and friendly. Church life was important to both of them, and they were members of their local church.

John Cotton was a church pastor in a town near Alford. He was a Puritan who had the charisma and zeal to arouse his listeners as no other had ever done. Anne was an ardent admirer of Mr. Cotton, who reminded her of her father.

The Reverend Cotton lived about 24 miles from Alford, and Anne and William went to hear him preach at every opportunity. As Anne traded in local markets or visited with friends, she heard only complimentary remarks about Cotton and praise for his teachings.

Before long, Anne began holding Bible studies in her own home for her friends and neighbors. Anne was well educated in the Scriptures from her father's teachings, and she also used the Reverend Cotton's sermons as a basis for some of her studies.

Anne gave birth to a new little Hutchinson about every year, reaching a total of 12 children by 1630. They were Edward, Susanna, Richard, Faith, Bridget, Frances, Elizabeth, William, Samuel, Anne, Mary and Katherine.

She had begun practicing midwifery in Alford, and with all her responsibilities, Anne's life was filled with duties.

Anne and William had lived a happy, contented life together, but William's business affairs began to deteriorate after the heavy taxation imposed by the new king, Charles I. Matters were complicated when the region suffered severe drought, followed by flooding.

Young William Hutchinson had died in infancy, and two of Anne's daughters, Susanna and Elizabeth, died in an epidemic of 1630. Anne and William began to seriously consider emigrating to the New World.

Another son was born in 1631 and was named William for his dead brother, and a daughter born in 1633 was named Susanna for her deceased sister. It was a custom of the time.

The Reverend Mr. Cotton had left England to go to the Massachusetts Bay colony a few weeks earlier, and the Hutchinsons had few people to console them in the deaths of their children. It was a widely held belief at that time that children's deaths were punishment for sins of the parents. Anne could not and would not accept this teaching. The couple decided to leave England and strike out for the colonies.

They obtained all the information they could from those already in Virginia and Massachusetts colonies. These glowing reports about how much better life was in the New World convinced them they had reached the right decision.

William turned his business over to a younger brother, while Anne awaited the birth of their fourteenth child, the second Susanna. After the birth, the family set out, boarding a ship, the *Griffin*, bound for Boston.

The Hutchinson family was at sea for about nine weeks, along with 90 other passengers, a crew of 50 and a cargo that included 100 heads of cattle consigned to Governor John Winthrop.

The smells of so many people crowded together on the ship, along with the odors from the cattle, were overpowering. Tempers flared as exhaustion increased.

One of the passengers, a preacher named Zechariah Symmes, insisted on delivering a five-hour nonstop sermon during the voyage. When he finally finished, Anne denounced his views in clear, ringing tones to the other passengers.

When the ship docked at Boston on September 18, 1634, the Reverend Symmes considered it his Christian duty to warn local church officials that Anne was a troublemaker. As a result, William Hutchinson was admitted to church membership immediately but Anne had to undergo a full week of questioning about her beliefs. She was afterward admitted as a member.

The Hutchinsons stayed with friends for a few months while their house was being built, and when they did move, it was to a smaller house than the one they had left in England. It was of the same type of construction as their former house, but not as well furnished, as they had been able to bring with them only the most necessary items.

Their new home was located across the road from that of Governor John Winthrop and his wife, Margaret.

In 1634, the year of their arrival, the General Court in Massachusetts issued the following order:

> That no person either man or woman shall hereafter make or buy any apparel, either woolen or silk or linen with any lace on it, silver, gold or thread, under the penalty of forfeiture of said clothes. Also that no person, either man or woman, shall make or buy any slashed clothes other than one slash in each sleeve and another in the back; also all cut-works, embroideries, or needlework cap, bands and rails are forbidden hereafter to be made and worn under the aforesaid penalty; also all gold and silver girdles, hatbands, belts, ruffs, beaver hats are prohibited to be bought and worn hereafter.

Anne had come to the New World to escape the tyranny of government, and she resented finding a similar situation in Massachusetts.

Two of William's aunts had come with the Hutchinsons to Massachusetts, and these ladies and the older Hutchinson daughters did much of the housework, leaving Anne with free time.

Anne decided to begin holding gatherings for women in her Bay colony home to discuss religion, as she had in Alford. The meetings would also serve to give women a time to visit with each other and relieve some of the intense loneliness they felt since moving so far away from relatives in England.

The Reverend John Cotton was now a teaching pastor in the church in the Massachusetts Bay colony, and Anne continued to review his sermons and expound the religious beliefs he taught.

Anne's meetings were well attended, and soon included most of the women living within traveling distance. Governor Winthrop did not become alarmed about Anne's teachings until men began attending the gatherings.

Governor Winthrop and other officials were attempting to impose the same type of wage and price controls on the businessmen in Massachusetts as those in England. The businessmen, however, had not left England to keep things the same, they wanted the freedom to operate their enterprises on the principles of supply and demand. William Hutchinson, as a textile dealer, understood their concerns.

William and two other men were asked to serve as a committee to negotiate with the Winthrop government to stop such proposals from becoming laws. The concerns of the businessmen were discussed in the Hutchinson home also.

The Reverend Cotton took no part in Anne's gatherings, even though they endorsed his views. He preferred to remain secluded from his devoted followers, spending, instead, 12 hours a day in religious studies. Anne approved of any seclusion Cotton sought if he felt it was necessary for his powerful ministry.

As attendance to Anne's meetings increased from 40 to 60 to 80, Governor Winthrop and the Reverend Thomas Weld, another Bay colony pastor, became alarmed. If this trend continued, there would be no limit to the power the Hutchinsons could exert in the colony.

Because the practice of midwifery was so little understood by men of that time, Anne's critics decided to fasten on her proven talents as a midwife to indicate she was evil, and possibly even a witch.

Anne not only served as a midwife for her neighbors, she also treated sick colonists with herbal remedies. Her patients had a much higher recovery rate than the patients of male physicians.

Since other medical practitioners in the area relied on such remedies as milk in which a tomcat's ear had bled for treatment of nervous prostration, and for a difficult labor a remedy involving chopped human hair and ants' eggs, Anne's herbal nostrums must have seemed to be on the cutting edge of scientific achievement!

Governor Winthrop feared a possible revolt by local businessmen. He had staked his entire fortune on the success of the colony, and he could not afford widespread dissension. Also, word of a potential uprising might come to the attention of the Crown, and Winthrop wanted to avoid this at all cost. He did not want the King's soldiers occupying Boston to keep order.

He became obsessed with driving Anne Hutchinson out of the colony, for he knew if Anne left, William would go also.

Anne and Margaret Winthrop had been good friends since they first met as neighbors, and Margaret became distressed as the enmity between her husband and friends increased. Anne had been a confidant when Margaret sorely needed someone in whom she could confide. Anne and Margaret had both lost children, and when Margaret grieved, Anne really knew how she felt. Margaret worried about where her duty lay in this serious controversy.

William Hutchinson had been making steady advances on the political front, and Anne was genuinely pleased by William's successes. He was elected deputy to the General Court in 1635, and later was elected to serve as a Boston selectman. He was an appraiser (judge) in small claims court. He had begun making investments in other businesses in the colony and had invested in land in the area.

In October 1635, young Henry Vane came to Boston. He was the 22-year-old son of King Charles's ambassador, Sir Henry Vane. Young Henry was a highborn aristocrat, but he had a reputation as a rebellious troublemaker. Nevertheless, Governor Winthrop welcomed him to Boston in the hope his presence might keep the King from rescinding the Massachusetts charter.

That same year the Reverend John Wilson returned from England to share the pulpit with the Reverend Cotton. Anne was amazed by the differences in the two ministers. The Reverend Cotton believed in a Covenant of Grace, the Reverend Wilson, in a Covenant of Works. Anne redoubled her efforts to convince her fellow worshippers that Wilson was wrong.

To Governor Winthrop's surprise and dismay, young Henry Vane allied himself with the followers of Anne Hutchinson. To add insult to injury, just seven months after young Henry's arrival in Boston, he was elected governor of the colony, replacing Governor Winthrop.

John Winthrop blamed Anne for his defeat in the election for governor. When she proposed the installation of her brother-in-law, John Wheelwright, as teaching pastor of the Boston church, Winthrop managed to prevent his appointment from being made.

Anne had a few other things on her mind at the time, as she gave birth to another son in 1636, whom they named Zuriel.

When the Pequot War started, Anne and her friends refused to become involved in fighting with the Indians. By the time it ended in July 1637, every Pequot had died in the war.

All the turmoil in Boston completely overwhelmed young Henry Vane and he returned to England. John Winthrop was re-elected governor after Vane left.

Apparently, Vane reported to the King about disharmony between the two religious factions in Boston, and the King decided to impose full British rule on the colony. He sent replacements from England for local officials. Governor Winthrop blamed Anne's interference in colony affairs for the King's actions and decided she must be stopped.

A religious synod was called for the end of August 1637. Church officials forbade Anne to hold any more meetings in the interim, and she was required to appear later in General Court to answer to charges of disrespect for the colony authority.

Anne was finally brought to trial before 49 legislators on a cold, gray November day in 1638. She was 47 years old and pregnant again.

Since her accusers were also her judges, she had no possibility of receiving a fair hearing.

Anne was subjected to close questioning by Governor Winthrop, who could not conceal his hostility toward her. He was unable to shake her testimony about biblical teachings, and she often matched him verse for verse in quoting Scriptures to support and counter the charges against her.

Finally, Governor Winthrop told her in icy tones, "We do not mean to discourse with those of your sex but only this; you do endeavor to set forward this faction and so you do dishonor us."

Governor Winthrop might have been called the father of New England by some historians, but among Anne's followers he was called, contemptuously, "Moses, the Lawgiver."

The legislators insisted Anne included men in her instructional meetings, and told her this was forbidden by church policies. She replied, "I call them not, but if they come to me I may instruct them."

Governor Winthrop found it impossible to hold his own with quick-witted Anne, whose father had instructed her so thoroughly in her childhood. When the governor asked her where she found authority in the Bible for her right to instruct men, she asked, "Must I show my name written therein?"

Anne's husband and her other relatives watched with dismay as the tide of public opinion slowly turned against her. When the trial started, she had hoped for support from both Governor Winthrop and the Reverend Cotton since she had served as midwife for both of their wives. Instead she met only cold resistance and enumeration of her errors, including the secret burial of the badly deformed stillborn baby born to Mary and William Dyer of Boston.

Anne was forced to stand for long hours in a bitterly cold room and face her accusers day after day. At last she almost collapsed, and a chair was brought for her.

After the hearing ended, Anne was banished from the Massachusetts Bay colony, and all her male supporters were ordered to surrender their arms and ammunition. Even the Reverend Cotton, upon seeing that public opinion was against Anne, voted for her banishment. In fact, a few weeks later Cotton was Anne's chief accuser in her excommunication trial at the Boston church. By this time Anne no longer cared whether she was excommunicated. She was only waiting for the hearings to end so she could join her husband and children in Rhode Island, where he was already making preparations for the establishment of a new home for them there on the island of Aquidneck.

Anne was excommunicated after lengthy debates. As she walked out of the hearing in silence, young Mary Dyer rose from her seat, held out her hand to Anne, and they walked out together into the cold air.

All the turmoil and nervous tension occasioned by the hearings caused Anne to suffer a miscarriage. The embryo had developed into a hydatidiform mole, an aberration that is usually precancerous.

Anne joined her family at Aquidneck in Narragansett Bay in March 1638. By March 1639, Anne was teaching in Rhode Island and continued to win many converts to her beliefs that God loved men and women equally and that works were not needed for a person to receive salvation.

Massachusetts authorities were wild with frustration in their inability to stop Anne's actions. Eighty other families had joined the Hutchinsons in their new location, and William Coddington was acting governor of the new colony.

Three years later William Hutchinson died, and Anne was deeply grieved. As soon as she could, she moved her six children still living at home farther down the coast to Long Island, in the New Netherlands colony, in an attempt to escape endless persecution by Massachusetts officials.

In 1643, Anne and five of her children were massacred by Indians. Her 10-year-old daughter, Susanna, was held captive by Indians for four years until a large ransom was paid to her captors by Hutchinson friends.

It is ironic that Indians should be the cause of Anne's death, since she and her friends had refused to fight them several years before.

Bibliography

Bremer, Francis J., ed. *Anne Hutchinson: Troubler of the Puritan Zion*. Huntington, New York: Robert E. Krieger, 1981.

Battis, Emery. *Anne Hutchinson*. Cambridge, Mass.: Harvard University Press, Belknap Press, 1971.

Morison, Samuel Eliot. *Builders of the Bay Colony*. Boston: Houghton Mifflin, 1964.

Williams, Selma R. *Divine Rebel: The Life of Anne Marbury Hutchinson*. New York: Holt, 1981.

6

Mary Barrett Dyer

In October 1637, while Anne Hutchinson awaited trial in Boston for her controversial religious views, she was asked by a friend and fellow midwife, Jane Hawkins, to assist at the birth of a baby born to young Mary Dyer, wife of the local hatmaker.

Mary and her husband, William, had not been living long in the Massachusetts area. Born in England, Mary Barrett had married William Dyer in London on October 27, 1633, in Saint Martin's in the Fields Church there. He made hats and was a Puritan, and on December 13, 1635, they had been admitted to membership of the Boston Church a few months after their arrival.

Mary had become a friend and follower of Anne Hutchinson and had attended religious gatherings held in Anne's home.

The present pregnancy, Mary's third in four years, was proving difficult. Her labor had begun two months early and the pain was excruciating. Despite all the best efforts of the midwives, Mary's baby was stillborn and was badly deformed. The women felt they should not let Mary see the baby in her weakened state after the difficult delivery, during which she had lost consciousness several times.

Anne and Jane were uncertain about the course they should follow in this new country, so Anne went to her friend, the Reverend John Cotton, for advice.

He told Anne that she and Jane should bury the baby as they

would have in England and that they should say nothing about it to anyone. Since Anne trusted Cotton, they buried the baby as he had suggested.

Later when Anne was brought to trial, William Dyer attempted to testify as a witness in her behalf. But Governor John Winthrop dismissed William as being "very apt to meddle in public affairs beyond (his) calling and skills."

William was disenfranchised, as were other male friends of the Hutchinsons.

As Anne left the scene of her trial, Mary Dyer got up from her own seat, and the two walked out of the building together, holding hands.

When Anne and her family left Boston, after Anne's banishment from the colony, Mary and William Dyer were excommunicated from the church, and they left the area also. They went to Aquidneck Island in the Rhode Island vicinity where William Hutchinson had gone earlier to get a house ready for his family.

Five days later Governor Winthrop had the body of Mary's baby exhumed. He wrote to preacher Roger Williams about the appearance of the child, describing its deformity, and he claimed it was caused by Mary's interest in Anne's teachings.

After the Dyers had lived on Aquidneck Island for a year, the continual bickering and quarrels among their neighbors became unendurable to them, and they moved on to help establish a new settlement at Newport, Rhode Island.

In Newport the Dyers found their real home, and over the next 15 years or so they added several more children to their family. Five sons lived beyond infancy. They were Samuel, William, Mahershallalhasbaz, Henry and Charles.

Mary's husband and children received her full attention during these years, even as she thought often of the extreme persecution suffered by her friend, Anne Hutchinson. Her husband was active in the colony and served in various positions in the government of Rhode Island colony.

Mary was a happy, serene individual by nature, and as she aged, she became increasingly dissatisfied with the Calvinistic doctrines of the Separatist faith.

In 1652 Roger Williams and John Clarke went to England to obtain confirmation of the charter for the landowners in Rhode Island and Aquidneck Island, and the Dyers went with them. Mary took her family, including her husband, to visit her aging mother, still living in England. While there, Mary became interested in the Quaker religious movement, then gaining strength in England. She became a follower of George Fox, leader of the Society of Friends.

A year later, Mary Dyer adopted the Quaker beliefs and spent several months traveling about England as a member of a Quaker evangelizing party known as the First Publishers of Truth.

Women were given important roles in the Quaker organization, completely different from the subordinate role assigned to women by the Church of England, the Puritans and the Separatists. Since the Quakers believed their God lived in the individual, they felt a woman as well as a man could be called to be a minister by the Inner Light. At first Quaker financial affairs were conducted by men, but women soon assumed the task of overseeing charitable projects, including the finances. Both sexes enjoyed equal membership status in the organization.

When Mary returned to Boston in 1657, after a five-year stay in England, she tried to tell her old friends about the Quaker doctrine — and she was promptly thrown in jail. A law had been passed allowing the imprisonment of "the cursed sect of heretics ... commonly called Quakers."

After her release from prison, Mary returned to her home on Aquidneck Island and started a Quaker meeting group among her friends and neighbors.

Soon other New England colonies, particularly Massachusetts, were pleading with government officials in Rhode Island to stop the Quaker movement from spreading. Mary was expelled from the New

Haven, Connecticut, colony when she promoted the Quaker cause there in 1653.

Rhode Island officials refused to take any action concerning Mary or her converts, saying, "We have no law among us whereby to punish any for only declaring by words their minds and understandings concerning the thing and ways of God, as to salvation and an eternal condition."

Mary felt compelled to return to Boston again and again to tell others of the Quaker movement, until at last she was sentenced to die by hanging. She wrote to the magistrates in Boston: "In love and meekness I beseech you to repeal these cruel laws, to stay this wicked sentence. ... But if one of us must die that others may live, let me be the one; for if my life were freely granted by you, I could not accept it as long as my sisters suffered and my brothers died. For what is life compared with the witness of Truth?"

Plymouth citizens watched in dismay as Boston officials continued to mistreat Quakers. An old man, Nicholas Upshall, who had lived a sober, blameless life, cautioned Massachusetts authorities that their abuse and mistreatment of the Quakers might lead to a judgment from God on Massachusetts. The officials responded by putting Upshall in jail, and they later banished him from Boston. With nowhere to go, he sought refuge with nearby Indians, who sheltered him from the winter cold and fed him. "What a God have the English who deal so with one another about the worship of their God," the chief of the Indian tribe remarked to Upshall.

On October 19, 1658, Massachusetts government officials enacted a law that authorized officials to banish Quakers, or even put them to death. In Boston several Quakers had already been banished with their sentence of death commuted so long as they stayed out of the city; now such punishment was applicable to all.

On October 27, 1659, Mary Dyer and her friends went to Boston, where she was led to the gallows with two convicted men of Quaker faith. They were William Robinson and Marmaduke Stephenson.

Men beat drums along the way so the three could not speak to the crowd of bystanders.

They were all blindfolded, and the men were hanged, one on each side of Mary. A rope was put around Mary's neck, but at the last minute she was again reprieved and put in her husband's custody. Governor John Winthrop, Jr., of Connecticut, Governor Thomas Temple of Nova Scotia and Mary's son, William, had all pleaded with authorities to spare her life.

Boston authorities had hoped to scare Mary so she would end her missionary efforts on behalf of her Quaker friends, but they did not succeed. She went back to Rhode Island for a while, then on to Long Island where she insisted she must return to Boston to try to "get the wicked law repealed."

Mary went back to Boston the next spring, where she pleaded with General Court officials to repeal the harsh laws against the Quakers. She wrote:

> I have no self ends, the Lord knoweth, for if my life were freely granted by you, it would not avail me, nor could I expect it of you, so long as I should daily hear or see the sufferings of these people, my dear brethren and seed, with whom my life is bound up.... Were ever the like laws heard of among a people that profess Christ to come in the flesh.... Woe is me for you! Of whom take you counsel?... In love and in the spirit of meekness I again beseech you, for I have no enmity to the persons of any; but what you sow, that shall ye reap from Him, that will render to everyone according to the deeds done in the body, whether good or evil, even so be it.

> Saith
>
> Mary Dyer

Boston authorities did not heed her warnings, and Mary was hanged in Boston on June 1, 1660, even though her husband had beseeched the authorities to spare her life, and he told the authorities that he was not a Quaker but a Puritan, which was true.

Mary had refused to repent. "In obedience to the will of the Lord I came and in His will I abide faithful to the death," she told her accusers.

A Boston citizen said sarcastically, after Mary's death on the gallows, "She hangs there like a flag!" Reportedly her body was taken back to Rhode Island for burial by some of her Quaker friends.

It was not until King Charles II appointed a commission to investigate the persecution of Quakers in Massachusetts that the brutality stopped. This time the fear was felt by the authorities in Boston, who did not want royal interference in colonial affairs.

William Dyer lived until about 1685. An inventory of his and Mary's possessions at the time of his death showed books worth £25, clothing valued at £110, sword and spurs worth £70, silver spoons and tankards were valued at £355, other household items were valued at £612, making the estate worth $4,500 in today's money.

Samuel Dyer, one of Mary and William's sons, married Anne Hutchinson's granddaughter, also named Anne Hutchinson. Young Anne was the daughter of Edward Hutchinson, a leading business-man in Boston in the 1660s. Samuel died young, and he and his wife had no children.

In 1959, about three hundred years after her death, a statue of Mary Dyer was erected on the lawn of the State House in Boston. It still stands.

Bibliography

Tolles, Frederick. "Mary Dyer." In *Notable American Women.* Vol. 1. Mass.: Harvard University Press, Belknap Press, 1971.

Williams, Selma R. *Dementers Daughters.* New York: Atheneum, 1976.

_____. *Divine Rebel: The Life of Anne Marbury Hutchinson.* New York: Holt, 1981.

7

Lady Deborah Dunch Moody

Lady Deborah Dunch Moody was not one to let her gender stop her from pursuing her dream of establishing a colony in America where all citizens could worship in freedom and safety. It took her about 14 years to achieve her goal, but she persevered.

Deborah was born in Avebury in Wiltshire, England, to Walter and Deborah Pilkington Dunch on April 3, 1586, and was christened there in Saint Giles Church. The little girl grew up among relatives who, even though they were members of the royal circle in English society, believed extensive reform was needed in the Church of England. Deborah's grandfather, William Dunch, served as auditor of the Mint for several years during the reigns of King Henry VIII and King Edward VI.

Deborah's father was officially named a barrister-at-law at age 27, and in 1584 and 1588 he served as a member of Parliament for the Suffolk coastal town of Dunwich.

Deborah lived during a time of great changes. The printing press, gunpowder and glass for windows, for instance, were all invented during her lifetime. Deborah's home was a stone manor house with many windows, decorated chimneys and large terraces outside.

Deborah's father died in 1594, when Deborah was only eight years old, and her mother married Sir James Marvyn of Wiltshire, also a member of Parliament, in 1598. Because of Mrs. Dunch's inheritance from her husband, Sir James was able to preserve and improve his own home of Avebury Manor. While Deborah was taught social graces and to read and write, she was not expected to have or voice opinions about any serious subject. When King James VI of Scotland took the throne as King James I of Great Britain, Ireland and France, Deborah was aware of the injustice, but she said nothing.

King James was a tyrant but he did authorize a new translation of the Bible by 47 bishops and other church officials, which version gained wide acceptance among English-speaking people.

Members of the Catholic Church had been unhappy for years because one of their members did not occupy the British throne. As Deborah made plans to marry Henricus Moody, a 23-year-old soldier, Sir Guy Fawkes and some fellow Catholic conspirators loaded the cellars beneath the Parliament Building with 36 barrels of gunpowder, intending to kill as many members of Parliament as possible in an explosion.

The plot was foiled before it was scheduled to occur on November 5, 1605, when Parliament opened, and King James instituted punitive rules and regulations against Catholic believers. Deborah learned then how dangerous a mixture of religion and politics could be.

On November 30, 1605, Deborah and Henry's marriage banns were posted in Saint Mary Aldermary Church in London, and their wedding was held on January 20, 1606. On March 18 that same year, Henry was dubbed "Sir Henry" by the King and was granted a coat of arms. His new wife became by courtesy, Lady Deborah.

The Moody's first child, a son named Henry, was born on February 7, 1607. A daughter, Catherina, was born in 1608.

The family home was in Garsdon Manor, located on an estate of 200 acres. The property had once belonged to King Henry I and his wife, Queen Maud. The manor house had walls five feet thick and contained elaborately decorated ceiling and columns.

King James I named Sir Henry a baronet on March 11, 1621. Henry served in Parliament in 1625, 1626, 1628 and a part of 1629.

In 1617 young Henry Moody entered Magdalen Hall, the Oxford grammar school. It was the most prestigious grammar school in England and counted Prince Henry, son of King James I, among its former students. Young Henry Moody received his Bachelor's Degree from Oxford University on February 7, 1624, his eighteenth birthday.

Catherina Moody, Deborah's daughter, married John Snow on February 7, 1627, in Saint Gregory–by–Saint Paul Church in London.

King Charles I had become the King of England in 1625 when his father, King James I, died. King Charles was convinced he had total power over his subjects, refusing to recognize any limitation by Parliament.

Sir Henry Moody died at Garsdon Manor on April 23, 1629, and left no will. His son inherited the property, which was extensive, and he sold almost all of it, except Whitchurch Manor. Deborah would have use of the house for her lifetime and would receive rent. The Crown, however, stepped in, demanding taxes and levying fines because Sir Henry had died intestate. Deborah was forced out, and Whitchurch Manor had to be sold. What could she do? She had relatives among the Puritans, who were being cruelly treated by King Charles. Fortunately, perhaps, for Deborah, Charles had in 1629 granted the Puritans a charter to establish a colony in the New World believing that would end his Puritan problem. At the time, however, Lady Deborah could not bring herself to leave England. Even when John Winthrop and his party of colonists were preparing to leave, she still wavered. She was 43 years old and England was the only home she had ever known. Her children and all her memories were there. She went to live in London to be near friends and relatives.

In her grief, Deborah attended religious gatherings of Anabaptists, Quakers and other dissenting groups. When news of her activities reached official government ears, she was told she would have to leave London and go back to live in the countryside. Even so, Deborah was fortunate; other dissenters had their ears cut off, were fined heavily, were imprisoned, or were publicly whipped or hanged.

Deborah, feeling abandoned by her country, finally relented. She gathered her personal belongings and sailed to the New World. She arrived in New England sometime in June 1639, probably on the ship *James*. No close relative accompanied her.

Lady Deborah may have stayed in Boston for a time after her arrival, but she was known to be living in the village of Lynn, about ten miles away, in 1640. On May 14 that year the General Court granted her 400 acres in her own name.

An earlier arrival in the area, Sir John Humphrey, had built an elaborate rock farmhouse, which he named Swampscott. It was located near Deborah's land. When he decided to take his wife and children back to England to live in October 1641, Lady Deborah bought the house and 900 acres surrounding it for £1,100, which, according to her account, caused her to be "almost undone."

Since property and houses in the area generally sold for about £25, Lady Deborah may have been cheated, but she had, at last, a home of her own. She also kept the small house in Salem she had bought when she arrived.

The nearest settlement to Swampscott was Salem. She joined the Salem Church in May 1640, but she soon learned that there was no religious tolerance in Salem. Church members were told what to do and what to believe. Anyone who disagreed was put in stocks, whipped publicly, fined or even imprisoned. It was the same situation she had left in England, except now the punishments were being meted out by dissenters. Anne Hutchinson had been banished for life from the Boston colony two years earlier.

The winter of 1642 was unusually snowy and cold, and Deborah had much time to reflect on the present problems in her life. Even women's clothing was regulated in Salem, and finery of any type, even embroidery, could not be used. The wearing of short sleeves was forbidden, and the length of long sleeves was required to be 22½ inches.

The Quarterly Court voted in the early spring of 1643 to fine and evict Deborah from Salem. They had learned she did not consider infant baptism to be an ordinance of God. She was ex-communicated from the Salem church.

Taking what personal items she could, Deborah had her cattle and pigs put on board a boat, which set sail south. Other like-minded people, including John and Mary Tilton, William Thorne, Edward Browne and Richard Stout sailed with her.

They eventually arrived at the Providence colony of Roger Williams, who had been banned from Boston earlier for his religious views. They learned voting rights were being hotly disputed in that colony, however, and they sailed on.

In the New Haven colony Governor Eaton's wife, Anne, was making her dissenting opinions public, and since her husband held opposing views, turmoil raged.

Deborah and her companions continued on through Long Island Sound, entered "The Narrows" at Hell Gate and sailed down the East River, finally putting in to shore at the southern end of Manhattan Island, at the colony of New Amsterdam, or New Netherland.

Englishman Samuel Maverick was at a loss to understand the actions of the leaders of the Boston colony. He said on his return home, "Whereas they went over thither to injoy liberty of Conscience, in how high a measure have they denied it to others ... merely for differing in Judgment from them. ... witness that Honorable Lady, the Lady Deborah Moody and severalle with her, merely for declaring themselves moderate Anabaptists."

Peter Minuit, a Huguenot, had bought Manhattan from the Indians in 1626, and the colony now had about 100 homes in it, most of which were built by the earliest settlers who had come from Holland, and there was an operating windmill. The soil was fertile, and there was plenty of good water in rock springs.

Deborah found temporary lodging while she explored the area and learned more about the colonists. There were about 400 men living here, mostly Dutch, but also some English, French and Portuguese. They had an interest in fur trading, very profitable here, and most had emigrated to New Netherland because of religious persecution in their own countries.

The fort was poorly built, and a section of the wall was sometimes overturned by roving livestock. There was no school, but a male tutor taught some of the boys, and there were two churches — one for Dutch Reformed believers and the other for the general community. There were grog-shops or bars where alcohol and tobacco were sold.

The biggest problem with the colony was Governor Willem Kieft. He refused to allow a town council to be named, and he was both incompetent and unjust. A major uprising among the local Indians had occurred just before Deborah and her companions arrived. It was in retaliation to Governor Kieft's having ordered his soldiers to attack an Indian village and kill the inhabitants because an Indian had killed a settler.

Since the governor was neither just nor fair, Deborah did not think this colony could be her new home. She was now 57 years old and needed to settle down. She had failed to find a home in a settled colony. Maybe, she mused, she should start a colony of her own.

Governor Kieft had total control of property in the area, and she dreaded asking him for any favors. She talked instead with his English secretary, Lieutenant George Baxter. She found him to be in favor of her plans, and they worked out an agreement for Deborah to be granted a tract of uninhabited land on Long Island, not far away. An informal patent was granted to her in late June 1643. Her town would be named Gravesend, for Governor Kieft's hometown in Holland, *s'Gravensande*, meaning the counts' beach, where counts held court before they moved it to the Hague. (The area is now Brooklyn.)

Deborah's new patent included 7,000 acres of land with access to excellent harbors. She cautioned all the settlers going with her to deal fairly with the Canarsie Indians living in the area and to pay them for their homesite.

The settlers did pay, but trouble came because the Indians thought the settlers were buying hunting and fishing rights to the property. The concept of total ownership and control of land was not known to them. They believed the earth belonged to everyone.

Young Penelope Van Princis came to live with Lady Deborah in 1643 after Penelope was released from Indian captivity. Richard Stout, a longtime friend and supporter of Lady Deborah, married Penelope a few months later. Deborah was delighted by their romance and enjoyed having them living nearby.

Deborah had taken her pigs with her when she left New Amsterdam colony, and they roamed freely on her property on Long Island. On December 19, 1645, Governor Willem Kieft granted her and some associates an official patent for Gravesend. It covered what is today Coney Island, Bensonhurst, Brighton Beach, Manhattan Beach, Unionville, South Greenfield and a part of Brooklyn.

Along with the patent, Deborah and her fellow colonists were granted freedom of conscience to form their own government and to make civil ordinances as they saw fit.

When an Indian attack occurred at Gravesend not long after the village was settled, her friends and fellow settlers managed to repel the invaders. They used Lady Deborah's substantial house as their fort.

Deborah considered returning to Massachusetts but was not encouraged to do so by either Governor John Winthrop or John Endicott, who termed her "a dangerous woman." Endicott recommended she not be allowed to return unless "she will acknowledge her evil in opposing the churches and leave her opinions behind her."

Gravesend citizens were forced to turn to farming to earn their living when their harbor proved to be too shallow to handle the anchorage of large ships. The colony was laid out in squares of 16 acres, divided into four squares of four acres each, on which homes were built — ten per four acres. A large road surrounded each 16 acre lot.

A wooden palisaded fence about 20 feet high surrounded the town for protection from wild animals and surprise attacks by Indians. Each settler had to help maintain the fence and keep a gun and ammunition readily available at all times.

Planter's lots were allotted to householders for gardens. These were outside the residential area and were also fenced.

Church attendance was left to the discretion of each individual, but in an attempt to teach responsible citizenship, attendance at town meetings was required. Penalty for nonattendance was a fine of five guilders.

There was no official church in Gravesend. Some settlers attended the Dutch Reformed Church in New Amsterdam, but Deborah and many others generally met in a private home where one person would read a passage from the Bible, followed by a discussion of the passage read.

Governor Kieft was recalled to Holland by the Dutch government in 1647, and Peter Stuyvesant was named to be the new governor of New Amsterdam. He and his wife Judith and his sister Anna Varleth, accompanied by her four children, arrived in New Amsterdam on May 11, 1647.

Governor Stuyvesant had more governing ability than his predecessor, but he also had a quick temper. His punishments included branding and piercing tongues with a hot iron and public whipping. To Lady Deborah's dismay, she learned Governor Stuyvesant considered himself the head of the Dutch Reformed Church. In his role as church leader, he had churches built in the area, procured ministers and generally supervised all the church affairs. If parents refused to have their children baptized, the parents were put in prison.

Governor Stuyvesant then began visiting all the nearby colonies, and finally he and his wife called on Deborah at Gravesend. Judith Stuyvesant was a well-bred, beautifully dressed woman with whom Deborah established a friendship. Both women loved music, and often Deborah would play her harp while Judith sang.

The Stuyvesants stayed several days with Deborah, and she was careful to guard her tongue on the subject of religion. She did not want any trouble with Stuyvesant, as she knew she might need his help sometime. The visit was satisfactory to everyone.

In 1649 Deborah rented her farming acreage to a tenant, Thomas Cornwell, turning her attention to selling the property she still owned in Massachusetts. The roof of her house in Salem had been blown off in a violent storm in 1646, and other problems arose. Living 200 miles away was too far for an absentee landlord.

She sold the property to Daniell King, a local merchant who, taking advantage of Deborah's distance from the property, made no payments for over five years. She then wrote him a letter in which she requested merchandise in lieu of payment. There is no record of her receiving anything at all from King.

Deborah was delighted when her son, Sir Henry II, arrived in Long Island in June 1650. Young Henry, a lawyer, had been a loyal subject of King Charles I, and he had used most of his money to support the king in his attempt to retain power in England. Parliament, however, ruled that all supporters of the king would have their property confiscated, and Henry was required to make a pledge never to bear arms against foes of the king.

In the New World, Henry turned his attention to gaining just payment from Daniell King for the Swampscott property Deborah had sold him years earlier. She finally received £105 total for the property, far less than she paid originally.

In 1651 Indians attacked Gravesend again, and this time the citizens sent a formal protest to the Dutch West India Company in Amsterdam about their practice of selling muskets, powder and lead indiscriminately to the Indians. They told the officials of the company that the whole area of New Netherlands would be destroyed and the white inhabitants killed by Indians if the arms sales were not halted.

When war between England and Holland started the next year,

the English residents at Gravesend were suspected of espionage. Even though a document had been signed every year for the past several years vowing support for Governor Stuyvesant, all Dutch colonists' support and interest evaporated.

Governor Stuyvesant learned of the Gravesend's citizens dissatisfaction with his lax control of law enforcement and general neglect of the colony. He decided to appeal to Lady Deborah to help him regain the respect he had formerly enjoyed in Gravesend.

They met at Lady Deborah's home on November 23, 1654. Two of the governor's council members went with him. Most of the Gravesend citizens also attended the meeting to tell the governor that they wanted their elected magistrates to be certified by him as officials. Promising that the magistrates would continue in office, Governor Stuyvesant left, telling the people "to fear God, honor their magistrates and obey both."

When English settlers tried to overthrow Dutch rule in New Amsterdam, Lady Deborah was distressed. She had obtained her patent from the Dutch, and they had allowed her and the other citizens to handle religious beliefs in their own way. She feared if England ruled the Gravesend area, they would try to force religious rules and practices on the colonists. But Governor Stuyvesant and his supporters had always ruled harshly, and in 1656 they began to rule religious observances also. Sabbath observance was enforced, taverns were closed and games were forbidden. New arrivals who belonged to other than Dutch Reformed groups did not find a welcome in New Amsterdam.

Lady Deborah had always welcomed all religious factions, and everyone had lived in harmony. She believed in "More praying and less preaching."

In Boston Quakers were still being treated brutally. They were flogged, fined and imprisoned for allowing meetings to be held in their own homes. When some Quakers came to Gravesend in 1657, Governor Stuyvesant also reacted negatively, and they were treated as badly as they had been in Massachusetts. Deborah, however, welcomed the Quakers and they began a ministry in her home. It was reported, but never proven, that she converted to Quakerism.

Deborah was discouraged. Religious freedom that she had sought for everyone in Gravesend was over. Her health had deteriorated from the intense stress she had endured for the past two years, and she died in early spring of 1658. She was buried at Gravesend.

Sir Henry Moody left Gravesend after his mother's death, and he sold her property to Jan Jansen Verryn. Later he had to sue Verryn for failure to pay for the land. When Verryn was then unable to pay, the title reverted back to Sir Henry.

In 1660 Henry went to Virginia as an ambassador from New Netherland, and later that year he resold his mother's property to John Bowne on September 6.

Sir Henry never married and never returned to Gravesend. He died about 1661 at the home of Virginia Colonel William Morrison, and was probably buried in Virginia. His baronetcy ended at his death since he had no son to inherit the title.

Bibliography

Cooper, Victor. *A Dangerous Woman: New York's First Lady Liberty.* Bowie, Md.: Heritage, 1995.

Earle, Alice Morse. *Colonial Dames and Good Wives.* New York: Frederick Unger, 1962.

Newman, Daisy. *A Procession of Friends.* Garden City, N.Y.: Doubleday, 1972.

8

Penelope Van Princis Stout

If Penelope Van Princis had known the troubles she would face when she came to the New World, probably she would have decided to stay in her Amsterdam home where she had been born about 1622.

In 1642, shortly after her ill-fated voyage, Penelope was married to Kent Van Princis. She was 20. After their wedding, they decided to emigrate to the American colony of New Amsterdam, which had been established by fellow Dutchmen. There, they had been told, they could prosper more than in Europe.

The ship on which they sailed wrecked upon their arrival in the Sandy Hook area of New Jersey, and Penelope's husband was seriously injured. The other passengers on the ship and the ship's crew decided to go on to New Amsterdam on foot, as they feared an Indian attack in the desolate, remote area where the ship had run aground. Penelope's injured husband could not possibly walk anywhere, and she elected to stay with him. Their fellow passengers left, promising they would send help back to the stranded couple.

Their companions had been gone only a few hours when a party of Indians attacked Penelope and her disabled husband. Kent was killed and Penelope seriously wounded. She knew her only hope of survival was making the Indians think she had died also, so she lay as lifeless and motionless as she could.

She was in serious condition, with her skull fractured, her

shoulder hacked with a hatchet and extensive abdominal wounds. She was, in fact, near death.

The Indians thought she had died and ignored her as they prepared their evening meal.

After the Indians left, Penelope, suffering excruciating pain and half-conscious from her injuries, decided she must seek some sort of shelter. When she tried to stand, however, she found she was unable. She had lost a great deal of blood from a large gash across her abdomen.

She crawled painfully across the ground, until she came to a hollow tree, and she took refuge in it. The tree trunk was cramped quarters for Penelope, but it was protection. When she got cold during the night, she crawled back to fire the Indians had built and kept it going for warmth. Penelope had no food, and for the next several hours she ate moss and fungal growths on a tree to stay alive.

On the second day of her ordeal, two Indian braves came again into the area and found Penelope lying near the fire. They were surprised to find a wounded white woman alone on the beach, and she could tell from their conversation they did not know what to do with her.

Penelope lay wishing she had died during the first attack, for she was convinced she would be killed now. The younger Indian man came toward her with his tomahawk raised, but the other man was older, and he moved the brave aside and picked Penelope up in his arms. He carried her to their camp, across his shoulder as if he were carrying the carcass of a deer he had killed. In this manner he took Penelope to a wigwam in which some of the women and children of his tribe lived. There she was given food and water, and her wounds were treated.

Over the next several weeks as she slowly regained her health, Penelope lived in a wigwam as an Indian woman, pounding and pulverizing corn and cooking for the tribe. She was well-treated, but she longed to return to her own people.

As weeks passed, with no sign of rescue, Penelope resigned herself to spending the rest of her life with the Indians. There was no way she could escape, as she had no idea where she was or where she could find white colonists.

Even though there was often serious tension between the Indians and settlers, they still traded with each other and communicated. It was in this way the people in New Amsterdam learned where Penelope was living. When rescuers had come back for her earlier, she was not at the scene of the shipwreck, and they did not know where to look for her.

Men from New Amsterdam came to the Indian camp and demanded Penelope's release. The old Indian man who had saved Penelope's life asked her what she wanted to do. He assured her she was welcome to live with the Indians for the rest of her life, if that was what she wanted, or she could go live with the strangers who had abandoned her and her husband in their hour of need. Penelope thanked him for all the kindness he had shown her, but she told him she should go to live in New Amsterdam.

Lady Deborah Moody, an Englishwoman who was one of the settlers who had recently moved into the area, took Penelope into her home to live.

About a year after her return, Penelope married Richard Stout, an Englishman, on January 1, 1644. Richard was 40 years old and had served as a seaman on a man-of-war schooner for seven years after he left England, but he finally tired of the sea and he left his ship at New Amsterdam. He had lived first in Lynn, Massachusetts, where he became acquainted with Lady Moody. He had been born in Nottinghamshire in England.

Governor Willem Kieft had employed Richard to aid him during the 1643 Indian uprising and he was highly regarded in the colony.

Richard had come to New Amsterdam to live with the Dutch people and to escape the religious persecution inflicted on other colonists at the hands of the Puritans in Massachusetts. In 1641 he had visited Long Island, in the company of other men from Lynn and Ipswich areas of Massachusetts, and they were favorably impressed with the region.

Led by Lady Deborah Moody, Richard and 38 other colonists moved to settle a new area on Long Island in a colony known as Gravesend. He was deeded several acres of land around which he was required to maintain a fence.

Several years later, in 1664, Richard and Penelope went with their children and other English families to live in Middletown in the Monmouth area of New Jersey. All the discord between the colonists and Indians in Gravesend was unpleasant. Their new location was nearer the Indian village where Penelope had lived for two years.

Penelope's Indian friend who had saved her life years before came to visit her from time to time in her home. He was getting old, and he may have felt some responsibility for the young white woman he had saved from death at the hands of his people. Penelope and Richard had children, and the old Indian may have enjoyed playing with them or watching them play. Penelope welcomed his visits and often inquired about members of the tribe.

One day when he came to visit, he did not talk as much as he had previously, and Penelope asked him if he was sick. He did not answer immediately but kept his eyes fixed on the children as they played. Finally he told Penelope that his tribe planned to attack her village that night. He said all the houses would be burned, all the cattle would be taken, and probably most of the colonists would be killed. He told her he would also be killed if the other members of his tribe knew he had told Penelope of their plans, but he felt he had to warn her. He told Penelope he had hidden a canoe nearby, where she could get to it easily, and that she should go tell her husband, take her children and go back to New Amsterdam and safety as fast as she could.

Richard Stout was working out in a field with other men when she sent one of the children to tell him to come in to talk with her.

On hearing about the warning her friend had given her, Richard doubted the Indian's story. Richard told Penelope that the Indians and white people had good relations through their trading, and they had lived peacefully side by side for years now. Why would they decide suddenly to attack people who were not bothering them?

Penelope, having lived with the Indians, knew their way of thinking better than Richard did, so she told Richard she did believe her friend and she planned to take their children and leave. If Richard wanted to stay in Middletown and face a possible massacre, he could. She and the children were leaving in the canoe provided by her friend, and they would send help for him and the other settlers when they reached New Amsterdam.

Richard went on back to the field to work, and when he came back to the house late in the day, he found Penelope and their children gone. It was obvious Penelope believed the old man's warning, and Richard began to wonder if it might be wise to warn the other settlers, just in case.

Richard gathered the other men in the village as rapidly as he could and explained the situation. The other men were alarmed and voted to arm themselves and prepare for an attack. They moved all their wives and children to one house near the entrance to their village and made preparations to spend the night on watch.

About midnight, the settlers heard the dreaded Indian war whoops as the braves approached the village. They did not know what they should do—whether to begin firing and kill as many Indians as they could, or let them come into the village and surround them after they got inside.

They decided to try to talk to the Indians and see why they were attacking. Richard and the other men went out to meet the Indians, understanding the risk they were taking, but reasoning that they would also kill some of the braves if the Indians shot at them.

When the Indians saw the villagers were well armed with muskets and pistols, while they had only tomahawks, bows and arrows, and possibly one or two guns, they decided to see what the white men had to say before attacking. The Indians told the villagers that some of them had not been paid for land taken by some of the white settlers. A conference was arranged for the next day to iron out the conflict.

The next day the white settlers who had taken the land without paying for it agreed to pay the Indian owners the price they wanted, and a treaty was signed.

As soon as Richard could get a message to Penelope that the danger of an Indian attack was over, she and their children returned home.

Penelope's adventures did not seem to mar her health overall, although she bore the scars of her injuries all her life. She and Richard had a total of ten children over the years, seven sons and three daughters, and left many descendants.

Richard died at age 88 in 1692, and, according to reports, Penelope lived to be 110 years old, which would make the date of her death around 1732!

Bibliography

Cooper, Victor. *A Dangerous Woman.* Bowie, Md.: Heritage, 1995.

National Society of the Colonial Dames of America. *A Few Unsung Women, Colonial and Pioneer.* Wendell, N.C. Broadfoot's Bookmark, 1982.

Stockton, Frank R. *Stories of New Jersey.* New Brunswick, N.J.: Rutgers University Press, 1961.

9

Frances Culpeper Berkeley

Frances Culpeper had the distinction of marrying three colonial governors. Born in England in 1634, the daughter of Lord Thomas and Lady Kathryn Saint Leger Culpeper, she was educated in England.

Frances married her first husband, Samuel Stephens of Bolthorpe, Warwickshire, England, in 1652, when she was 18 years old. They were married in the Jamestown colony in Virginia where Frances and her father had been visiting since the year before. Lord Culpeper was one of the Virginia Company subscribers of the colony. Culpeper returned to England, but Frances remained in the New World with her husband. In 1667 Stephens was named the colonial governor of the Albemarle colony in North Carolina, and he and Frances lived there. He was the owner of nearby Roanoke Island.

Frances's life with Samuel Stephens was more orderly and serene than the lives of the first women colonists in the Massachusetts area. Her husband was a man of influence, and they had servants to do any household work that needed to be done. It was not necessary for Frances to do any cooking, laundry or gardening. There was abundant food and Frances had brought beautiful clothes with her.

Governor Stephens died in December 1669, and a few months later Frances married a second time. Her new husband was Governor William Berkeley, colonial leader of the Virginia colony. At age

36, Frances was much younger than Governor Berkeley, then 64 years old.

Governor Berkeley had come to Virginia in 1640 and was named governor of the colony in 1642. In 1646 he had a large brick mansion built for his home on a 1,000 acre tract of land, which he owned, near Jamestown. He called his property Green Springs Plantation.

Frances went to live in the mansion after their marriage. The home measured 100 feet across the front and had six large rooms and a central hall, which measured 48 feet wide and 43 feet long. There were two symmetrical wings on the building, which extended out 26 feet on either side.

A good road was built from Green Springs to Jamestown, the first capital of Virginia, and a quarter-mile of it was straight. After they had attended church on Sunday, Governor Berkeley and his friends began racing their carriage horses on the straight stretch of road, and the development of the "quarter horse" began. (Quarter horses run at high speeds for short sprints, but they don't have the stamina to run longer races.)

Governor Berkeley's first term in office, from 1642 to 1652, was successful. He was well regarded by Virginia colonists and other officials alike. He heard settlers' complaints and managed to put the interest and well-being of the colony ahead of his own. A number of vast estates developed in Virginia during this period. In England there was turmoil in the government, and the Cavaliers who emigrated to Virginia found a sympathetic governor.

The Cavaliers managed to assume full control of Virginia's government, which no longer recognized the votes of other citizens.

Governor Berkeley was forced from office from 1652 to 1659, when a British Naval fleet was sent to take control of Virginia while Cromwell was running the government in England. However, even before the King was restored to the throne in England, the Virginia House of Burgesses and Council asked William Berkeley to be governor of Virginia again. For the next ten years after he resumed his duties as governor, Berkeley was again in favor with most of the colonists.

After his marriage to Frances, his popularity began to wane. It was around Lady Frances, as she preferred to be called, that Virginia aristocratic society began to take form on American soil in 1670. She reigned queenlike from the Berkeley mansion at Green Springs. She received the wives and daughters of other wealthy planters in the area with an imperious manner, richly gowned and bejeweled.

One member of Frances' social group at Green Springs was Laetitia Corbin Lee, wife of Richard Lee II, also owner of a Virginia plantation. The Lees lived in a large brick mansion also, which boasted carpeted floors, elaborately carved and upholstered furniture, and heavy silver and gold ornaments. Mr. Lee's library was second to none in any of the colonies.

Other families living in the Jamestown area also owned large plantations, which they operated under feudal conditions. Many were Cavaliers who had supported King Charles I during his troubled reign in England, and they had been forced to leave after Cromwell became Lord Protector.

Tobacco was the money crop in Virginia, and all prices were given in pounds of tobacco. Even wealthy colonists used credit for purchases, and paid their bills when English officials sent them money for their tobacco crops that had been sold there. Some tobacco was sold to other European countries until 1665. After that time, England bought all tobacco and re-exported it in Europe by law.

All the plantation owners enjoyed their influence and power, but some of their attitudes and rules rubbed the owners of small farms in the region the wrong way. The farmers had not left England to become subjects of another feudal system in Virginia.

In some ways the Virginia aristocrats were pitiful. They were attempting to transplant to their new location the same English society with which they were familiar, being more comfortable in a society which had social classes and distinctions. The Green Springs society members not only occupied most important government posts in the Virginia government, they also controlled the local church and its affairs. All were members of the Anglican Church, and they had come to Virginia to escape persecution by Cromwell's forces — not for religious freedom. They did not adhere strictly to formal rituals of church worship, but the church was an important part of their lives.

In 1672 King Charles II complicated matters by granting Governor Berkeley permission to liquidate titles to land held by some farmers on smaller acreage. The governor could then include that land in proprietary grants to the king's supporters.

In addition to this unfair practice, the middle-class tobacco farmers believed Governor Berkeley did not give them adequate protection against Indian raids. They thought his failure to do so stemmed from his fear that the Indians would stop trading furs with him.

Nathaniel Bacon, a cousin of Lady Berkeley's, arrived in Virginia in 1674, and the Berkeleys entertained him in their home as a guest for a time until he bought a plantation some distance from Jamestown. Governor Berkeley tried to be supportive of Bacon and gave him an appointment to the Virginia government Council on March 3, 1675.

When Governor Berkeley refused Bacon a partnership in the lucrative Jamestown fur trading monopoly, however, the moody young settler began inciting the citizens to rebel against Berkeley's government. Bacon was a malcontent who had been sent to Virginia by his father after having been involved in an attempt to defraud one of his friends out of his legal inheritance. Governor Berkeley did not need Bacon to cause more trouble. Virginia was a difficult colony to govern because the settlers lived some distance from each other due to the sizes of their holdings. The church could not serve as a focal point for the community as it did in some colonies of the Northeast because of its distance from most of the members.

Bacon was aided, inadvertently, by Frances Berkeley's high-handed treatment of volunteers from New Kent who came to the governor in April 1676, offering to mobilize and fight for the colonists' protection during Indian raids. Governor Berkeley had made little effort to gain control of the Indians or to improve protection of colonists living in outlying districts. Berkeley told the volunteers that his regular militia could handle the Indians and refused the assistance of the volunteers. Frances didn't help matters when she asked the volunteers why they thought they would be more effective in fighting Indians than the militia would be.

Elizabeth Duke Bacon, Nathaniel's wife, and her friends spread the rumor that Governor Berkeley was an Indian supporter, and that added fuel to the flame.

Bacon began his campaign against Governor Berkeley by leading some of his fellow rebels in attacks on friendly Indian camps, despite the governor's orders to leave them alone.

On June 1, 1676, Governor Berkeley sent Frances to England on board the *Rebecca*, along with their gold and silver plate for safekeeping. He sent a letter by her to the secretary of state, Henry Coventry, in which he wrote, "Sir, I am so overwearied with riding into all parts of the country to stop this violent rebellion that I am not able to support myself at this age six months longer, and therefore on my knees I beg his sacred Majesty would send a more vigorous governor."

On June 12, 1676, Philip Ludwell, deputy secretary of the Virginia colony, wrote Lady Frances that Governor Berkeley had pardoned Bacon after she left, and that Bacon was planning to recruit volunteers to help him fight the Indians, who were not giving any trouble at the moment.

Frances Berkeley pled her husband's cause eloquently to King Charles, but rebel Bacon's female supporters were more effective in their presentation, and Governor Berkeley was censured by the king.

Bacon's wife argued that her husband's rebellion stemmed from the failure of Berkeley to protect settlers from Indian attacks, yet he would not give permission to her husband to do so.

On September 15, 1676, Nathaniel Bacon and his men attacked Jamestown with the intention of overthrowing the rule of Governor Berkeley. They burned homes, the church and the State House, effectively destroying the town four days later.

On September 20, Bacon took possession of Green Springs mansion for use as his headquarters. Governor Berkeley had to flee to an outlying estate of one of his supporters.

A month later, on October 26, 1676, Nathaniel Bacon died of "bloody flux." Joseph Ingram assumed leadership of the rebels, but the rebellion soon dwindled without Bacon to lead them.

Governor Berkeley returned to his Green Springs plantation on January 21, 1677. The mansion had been so badly damaged by the rebels, he had to borrow a bed from a neighbor so he could spend the night.

With the town of Jamestown destroyed, Green Springs became the headquarters of the colony government.

Frances Berkeley returned to Virginia on the *Rose* on February 11, 1677. She was accompanied by Herbert Jeffreys, a royal commissioner. They brought a thousand British soldiers with them to restore order in the Virginia colony.

When she saw the condition of the mansion at Green Springs, Frances wrote in a letter to her cousin, the wife of Sir Abstrupus Danby, that "it looked like one of those the boys pull down at Shrovetide, and was almost as much to repair as if it had beene new to build, and no sign that ever there had beene a fence about it...." In the same letter, Frances said she had spent £300 of her own money "to make it habitable, and if I had not bestowed that money upon it, the Plantation had not been worth One Hundred Pounds."

Governor Berkeley lamented in a letter to Thomas Ludwell, "How miserable that man is that Governes a People where six parts of seaven at least are Poore, Endebted, Discontented and Armed."

The King in England was inclined to be lenient with the rebel faction, and he sent a pardon for all of them except Nathaniel Bacon, who was now deceased.

Governor Berkeley protested that the rebels should be punished, as he and his supporters had suffered much damage and lost most of their possessions during the uprising of the rebels. The King replied by sending Colonel Herbert Jeffreys with Frances to Virginia to replace Governor Berkeley, and he sent a commission to hear complaints against Berkeley.

On April 27, 1677, Colonel Jeffreys proclaimed himself the governor of Virginia, and on May 13 that year, King Charles II ordered William Berkeley to return to England.

Peace treaties were signed with the Indians at Williamsburg on May 29, 1677.

Berkeley obeyed the King's order and arrived in England in June of 1677. Immediately, he petitioned the King to grant him a hearing of his side in the Virginia turmoil.

William Berkeley never got to have an audience with the King. He died on July 9, 1677, at age 71 and was buried in England.

Apparently Governor Berkeley had been happy in his marriage to Frances. He bequeathed all his property "to my dear and most virtuous wife and if God had blessed me with a far greater estate, I would have given it all to my most dearly beloved wife."

In fact, Lady Berkeley was left with an estate ruined as a result of the rebellion. The buildings were badly damaged or destroyed, furniture was damaged or missing, fences were down and the livestock was severely depleted.

The mansion had been repaired, and Frances, believing Green Springs the only estate fine enough for the home of a governor, planned to rent it to future governors. She hoped to return to England and use the rent to support herself.

Her plans did not materialize, and in 1680 Frances married Philip Ludwell, who was governor Berkeley's deputy secretary and a loyal supporter of the Governor during the rebellion.

The newlyweds went to London for a honeymoon and returned to live at Green Springs. Frances spent the winter of 1684 in England at Leeds's Castle, and she returned to England with her husband from time to time for official court appearances.

Philip Ludwell served as governor of the North Carolina colony from 1689 to 1693.

Frances died at Green Springs about 1695. Her grave is at Jamestown, but the inscription on the gravestone is barely legible.

Ludwell was governor of both of the Carolina colonies in 1693 and 1694. He appointed a deputy to govern North Carolina in 1694 and moved to Charleston to govern the southern colony for a time, finally returning to England to live.

Governor Ludwell had a son, Philip II, and a daughter by a previous marriage. Philip inherited the Green Springs property upon Governor Ludwell's death.

Williamsburg became the colonial capital of Virginia in 1703.

Bibliography

Talpalar, Morris. *The Sociology of Colonial Virginia.* New York: Philosophical Library Press, 1960.

Washburn, Wilcomb E. *The Governor and the Rebel.* Chapel Hill: University of North Carolina Press, 1957.

Webb, Stephen Saunders. *1676, the End of American Independence.* New York: Alfred A. Knopf, 1984.

10

Margaret Hardenbroeck Philipse

Margaret Hardenbroeck was born in the Rhine Valley of the Netherlands at Elberfeld about 1640, to Adolph Hardenbroeck and his wife, the former Maritje Caterberg. The Hardenbroecks also had an older son, Abel.

Margaret attended school in her village, and was evidently a good student, as she would become an international trader and ship owner when she became an adult.

In 1659 Abel Hardenbroeck agreed to emigrate to the New Amsterdam colony in America to serve as an indentured servant of the Ten Eyck family, and Margaret came with her brother.

On October 10, 1659, Margaret married a wealthy merchant trader named Pieter Rudolphus de Vries in New Amsterdam. Their first child, a daughter named Maria, was born about a year later and was baptized on October 3, 1660.

Margaret was hired to be a business agent for the Dutch merchants Wouter Valck, Daniel des Messieres, and others engaged in trading with colonists in New Netherlands. A Dutch deposition dated 1660 showed Margaret had a financial arrangement with Wouter Valck, which referred to her as "Margaret Hardenbroeck, living in the Manhattans in New Netherland who is at present married to Pieter Rudolphus (de Vries), merchant there." She sold pins, cooking oil and vinegar, and bought furs to send to Holland.

When Pieter Rudolphus de Vries died in 1661, Margaret took control of his business operations. She bought and shipped furs to Holland to pay for Dutch merchandise she bought to sell to colonists in New Amsterdam. She purchased a ship during this period named the *King Charles.* Dutch wives were gaining reputations as good businesswomen, but Margaret's international trading and serving as operator of a shipping service were unusual.

The arrival of Peter Stuyvesant in 1647 as colonial governor of New Netherlands marked a turning point for the better for the colony. He worked to bring a semblance of order to the sprawling, unruly colony, which had multiple ethnic factions and languages.

In 1653 Governor Stuyvesant had organized a municipal government for New Amsterdam, which had been constructed around a fort instead of around a church as most other New England colonies had been.

He established schools for both boys and girls in an effort to improve the religious and moral climates in the colony, the laxness of which distressed him. The teachers were ordered to give religious instruction before going on to instruction in "reading, writing, arithmetic and cyphering." The schools were free for poor children, but a nominal fee was paid by affluent parents.

When Margaret Hardenbroeck arrived in New Amsterdam in 1659, the colony was an odorous, filthy place, where hogs roamed freely in the streets and rooted holes in them. The owners of the hogs were ordered to put rings in the noses of the swine, and ruling councils considered barring hogs from the city unless they were kept in pens, but the proposal was not passed.

Privies discharged waste into the streets, and ashes, dead animals and garbage were thrown into the canal nearby. Epidemics of various diseases with fevers, chills and dysentery occurred frequently with tragic results.

Margaret's husband had possibly failed to pay suppliers or investors or employees, but for whatever reason, in the year following his death Margaret found herself enmeshed in many lawsuits involving his business enterprises.

During this turbulent period in her life, Margaret became romantically interested in a young man named Frederick Philipsen, who had worked as a carpenter, architect and business contractor for Governor Peter Stuyvesant's company. Now Philipsen had progressed to being an important person in the political and economic life of New Amsterdam.

In October 1662, banns of their marriage were published, and subsequently, the Court of Orphan Masters requested Margaret to present an inventory of her daughter Maria's inheritance from the father.

Margaret had a prenuptial agreement that Philipsen had signed, so the Court accepted the agreement in lieu of the requested inventory.

After their wedding, Philipsen adopted Maria, and her name was changed to Eva. Their home was located near the East River, facing Long Island.

The women in New Amsterdam were much more emancipated than those in other colonies, as they had enjoyed greater respect and had more personal and business rights in Holland than the women in England. Dutch women could own and operate businesses of their own, could make wills giving their property to anyone they chose, and could make legal contracts in their own names.

Margaret continued with her own business affairs after her marriage to Philipsen. Even though she gave birth to three sons and another daughter during the next several years, she also made ocean voyages between New Amsterdam and Holland. Legal documents showed her to be in Holland in January 1664, and from December 1668 to January 1669.

During the last mentioned trip, Margaret was one of the several merchants who petitioned the king of England to allow her ship, the *King Charles*, to sail from Amsterdam in Holland to New Amsterdam, now called New York. Permission was granted after several delays.

England's government officials had coveted New Amsterdam from its beginning. After an Indian invasion of the colony at the urging of the officials and later an invasion by British forces, New Amsterdam became New York officially on September 8, 1664, when Colonel Richard Nicolls led his English conquerors into the city. There were now about 300 buildings and 9,000 people living in the area. Most citizens stayed in the renamed colony as it had become their home. Governor Stuyvesant went to Holland to defend himself against charges that he was to blame for the conquest by the English. He was gone for three years.

Under laws now invoked by British officials, Margaret Philipsen could no longer buy or own property in her own name, nor transfer power of attorney to her husband. She had to defer to her husband in business matters, and they were no longer equal partners. Margaret was not happy about these restrictions as she knew she had competence in business affairs.

Frederick Philipsen swore allegiance to the king of England in 1664. When he was named to serve on the colonial council in 1674 by Governor Edmund Andros, he dropped the "n" from his last name to anglicize it, and again swore his allegiance to the king of England.

Homes and other buildings in New York were Dutch in style, most often built of stones or bricks, and many had tiled roofs. Such a custom meant there were far fewer devastating fires in New York than in other English colonies, where the buildings were usually built of wood with thatched roofs.

Frederick Philipse profited financially and socially from his marriage to Margaret. Perhaps she did not keep the fire burning on the hearth, but she kept the profits accumulating from her business activities.

Frederick dabbled in both shipping and the slave trade, and with the backing from Margaret's fortune, he was able to expand his business interests until he became one of the richest men in New York.

In 1679 Margaret was serving as super-cargo on her ship *King*

Charles on a voyage from Amsterdam to New York, which meant she was the business manager and person in complete charge of the voyage. Her second daughter, Annetje was on board with her mother. Probably the captain's wife and children were on board also. On merchant ships family members of the owner lived in the aft, or rear, of the ship below the quarter deck. There was a stairway or ladder from the deck to the living area. Any loose articles, such as pictures and rugs, had to be stored under bunks while at sea, but they could be used when at anchor. Meals on board ship were hearty and filling. Vegetables and salt-cured meats were used, with maybe a live pig or chickens on board for future meals. The sailors caught fish fresh from the sea to vary the diet. Family members ate together with the captain in the captain's quarters, and the sailors got their food at the door of the galley.

Jaspar Danckaerts and Peter Sluyter were passengers on a voyage when Margaret was super-cargo, and they left a written record of her thrifty nature in their journal. They were Labadist missionaries searching for a suitable location for a new Dutch colony. These men accused Margaret of having "unblushing avarice and excessive covetousness." On one occasion they wrote that Margaret insisted both her crew and passengers search for a mop that had probably fallen overboard. The missionaries wrote, "we, with all the rest must work fruitlessly for an hour or an hour and a half, and all that merely to satisfy and please the miserable covetousness of Margaret."

Margaret retired from sailing after the voyage was completed, and she may have been suffering from some illness that caused her unpleasant behavior. She died about 1691. She was a carryover from old traditions. In 1700 there were no women traders in New Amsterdam, as the settlers had adopted English customs.

Margaret's daughter Eva (Maria) married Jacobus Van Cortland, and young Annetje married Philip French, also a merchant trader. All of Margaret's sons — Philip, Adolph and Rombout — worked in shipping, but only Adolph became his father's partner. He was put in charge of the overseas trading venture after his father's death in 1702.

Frederick Philipse had remarried in 1692 to a wealthy widow named Catherine Van Cortland Dervall, and the next year colonial Governor Benjamin Fletcher granted him 96,000 acres of fertile land in the Hudson Valley. He had the Old Dutch Church of Sleepy Hollow built for his 200 tenant farmers on Philipsburg Manor in North Tarrytown. Adolph inherited all this property, as well, and Margaret was probably buried there.

Bibliography

Andres, Charles M. *The Colonial Period of American History.* New Haven, Conn.: Yale University Press, 1967.

Berkin, Carol. *First Generations.* New York: Hill and Wang, 1996.

Hawke, David. *The Colonial Experience.* Indianapolis: Bobbs Merrill, 1966.

Kammen, Michael. *Colonial New York: A History.* New York: Charles Scribner's Sons, 1975.

Neidle, Cecyle S. *America's Immigrant Women.* New York: Hippocrene Books, 1975.

11

Elizabeth Haddon Estaugh

There were few women to come to live in colonial America who established towns of their own, but Elizabeth Haddon did. The town of Haddonfield, named for its founder, is located in New Jersey, seven miles southeast of Philadelphia. The 1980 census showed a population of 12,337 for the town.

Elizabeth was born on May 25, 1680, in Southwark, London, England, to John and Elizabeth Clark Haddon. John Haddon was a blacksmith and manufacturer of ship anchors. The parents were of Quaker faith and attended the Horseley Down Meeting.

Elizabeth was educated in Quaker schools and reared in Quaker simplicity. As a child, Elizabeth heard William Penn, the Quaker leader, talk with her father about the wonderful possibilities awaiting colonists in the New World. Through Penn's influence, John Haddon invested in a plantation containing 8,000 acres in the area Penn had been settling with religious refugees and businessmen seeking greater economic opportunities. It was in Newton Township in West New Jersey.

Mr. Haddon meant to emigrate to his newly acquired property when he bought it, but his failing health and business interests in England made it impossible. His daughter Elizabeth had been anticipating their move to Penn's colony for months, and she begged her parents to allow her to go alone. She told them she felt a calling to go to the New World and establish a lodging house for traveling Quakers, and she hoped to serve as a physician for her neighbors and nearby Indians. Her parents protested, saying she was too young to undertake such a task, and they asked her to consider the matter carefully for three months, until spring arrived. During the time she waited, Elizabeth studied herbal medicine, and her parents realized Elizabeth was serious about pursuing her dreams. They agreed she could go to America.

They hired a widow, Hannah (last name unknown), as her companion, and provided them with two male servants. Upon their arrival in Philadelphia in 1701, they probably visited William Penn and his wife, then living at Pennsbury Manor.

After a few days, Elizabeth and her party crossed the Delaware River to go to the Francis Collins home in New Jersey, where living arrangements for Elizabeth and her servants would be provided while her house was completed.

Elizabeth was amazed to see some colonists living in caves that had been dug out in the banks along the river. They had no other place to live while they built houses.

It was apparent to Elizabeth that her life would be radically different from the luxury and comfort she had enjoyed in her parents' home in England. Here in New Jersey, houses were miles apart, wild animals and Indians roamed freely and were encountered unexpectedly, and transportation was provided by boats or by walking everywhere.

Elizabeth's experiences caught the imagination of the poet Henry Wadsworth Longfellow, and he wrote of her adventure in *Tales of a Wayside Inn*.

Upon reaching her father's property and moving into the house that had been completed there, Elizabeth and her servants planted corn and rye. In four months she was ready to receive Quaker guests.

In his poem, Longfellow wrote of the following weeks when winter closed in:

Ah, how short are the days! How soon the night overtakes us!
In the old country the twilight is longer, but here in the forest
Suddenly comes the dark, with hardly a pause in its coming,
Hardly a moment between the two lights, the day
and the lamplight;
Yet how grand is the winter! How spotless the snow is and perfect!

Elizabeth sat sewing in her kitchen on the snowy evenings while her maid, Hannah, prepared their supper.

Hannah could not help contrasting their life in England with that in New Jersey:

But the great Delaware River is not like the Thames....
Out of our upper windows in Rotherhithe Street in the Borough,
Crowded with masts and sails of vessels coming and going'
Here there is nothing but pines with patches of snow on their branches....

Hannah pitied their servant Joseph having to travel in the snow on a sled pulled by oxen.

"How in the world shall we get to Meeting on First Day?" she asked.

Elizabeth assured her there would be a way provided for them to go, and Hannah, reassured, continued setting the table with plates and cups for their evening meal. She poured boiling water in the earthen teapot so the tea could steep as she worked.

Elizabeth realized Joseph had been gone a long time, and she wondered why he had not yet returned. She had sent him into the nearby village to take food and clothing to some needy families, but he had been gone longer than usual. As she told Hannah, however,

The house is far from the village;
We should be lonely here, were it not for friends that in passing
Sometimes tarry o'ernight, and make us glad by their coming.

Hannah could not stop herself from saying,

Yea, they come and they tarry, as if the house were a tavern;
Open to all are its doors, and they come and go like the pigeons.

97

Elizabeth was amused by Hannah's vehemence, but she told Hannah that she was only distributing to the poor a part of what God had given to her.

> And to those of his service ...
> We must not grudge then to others
> Ever the cup of cold water, or crumbs
> that fall from our table....

As the women talked, they heard sleigh bells outside, and then two men talking as they approached the house. Elizabeth said, "It is Joseph come back, and I wonder what stranger is with him."

Hannah removed the tin lantern from its nail on the wall to meet the men and light their way near the door. Light shone through the holes that pierced the round lantern, which had a pointed top like a lighthouse roof.

When Hannah and the men came into the warm house, Elizabeth rose to greet their visitor:

> Quietly she gave him her hand, and said, "Thou art welcome,
>   John Estaugh."

Elizabeth had met John Estaugh at a May Meeting in London she had attended years before as a child with her parents.

John asked,

> "Dost thou remember me still, Elizabeth? After so many years have passed,
> It seemeth a wonderful thing that I find Thee...."

John was pleased to receive such a cordial welcome, and he told Elizabeth of his meeting her servant Joseph on his way back home from his errand of mercy to the village.

> "I saw in the snow-mist ... a wayfarer
> ... who paused and waited," John said.
> "So I greeted the man, and he mounted the
> sledge beside me,

And as we talked on the way he told me of
Thee and Thy homestead....
How being led by the Light of the Spirit ... Thou hadst come to
    this country,
And I remembered Thy name, and Thy father and mother in England,
And on my journey have stopped to see Thee, Elizabeth Haddon,
Wishing to strengthen thy hand in the labours of love thou art doing...."

Joseph was by the door, stamping his feet to get snow off his boots, and when he had finished, they all sat down together to eat the supper Hannah had cooked.

Afterward, Elizabeth explained to her visitor how she had been led to New Jersey to help feed and clothe the needy and to provide temporary lodging for missionaries of the Quaker faith.

John Estaugh spent the night in Elizabeth's home, and before he left the next morning, he assured her they would see each other again at the May Meeting.

Elizabeth's step was lighter and her heart sang through the rest of the long winter, according to Longfellow's poem.

At last spring arrived, and John Estaugh returned to Elizabeth's home, accompanied by other people. They would all attend the local May Meeting, as was their custom.

Elizabeth and Hannah fed all the travelers, and soon they were ready to go on to the meeting site. Elizabeth whispered to John she wished he could stay a little longer — she wanted to talk to him in private.

John stayed longer as she had asked, and she said, "I will no longer conceal what is laid upon me to tell thee; I have received a charge to love thee, John Estaugh!"

John was surprised that Elizabeth would admit her love for him when he had not mentioned anything of that sort to her. He told her,

"I have no light to lead me, no voice to direct me....
When the Lord's work is done ...
I will gather into the stillness ...
And listen and wait for His guidance."

John returned to England after the May Meeting, and while he was gone, he thought about Elizabeth, her kindness to him and the poor people to whom she gave food and clothing, her pleasant demeanor — and he felt a call to love her.

When he returned to New Jersey, John came to see Elizabeth and told her he believed they should be married. They went to the Quaker Meeting, and in Silent Assembly, they clasped hands and promised each other "to be kind and true and faithful in all things." As was the custom of Quaker believers, no minister officiated at the simple ceremony.

Among the guests at the ceremony were local Indians and the governor of West Jersey. Their vows were exchanged on December 1, 1702, and by law John became the legal manager and lawful attorney of the Haddon properties, totaling 8,000 acres.

John's health was poor, so Elizabeth continued taking care of their business affairs as she had before her marriage. John continued with his ministry after their marriage also, and he traveled through the American colonies, then on to England, Ireland and the West Indies, telling people of his faith.

Through the years Elizabeth realized her dream to serve as a doctor to her neighbors and local Indians. John joined her in the ministry of medical care when he was at home, as he had studied both medicine and chemistry.

The "Brew House" where they prepared their medicines still stands in Haddonfield, the town they founded in 1713 when they built a new house there. Elizabeth's knowledge is shown by a salve she developed to heal skin sores. It was still being used 100 years later.

Elizabeth and John never had any children, and on one of the three visits she made to England, Elizabeth brought a young niece back with her when she returned to Haddonfield. The niece returned to England after spending a few months in America.

On another trip to England, in 1723, Elizabeth brought back her nephew, Ebenezar Hopkins, whom they adopted. Ebenezar was the son of Elizabeth's sister, Sarah Hopkins.

Ebenezar stayed in New Jersey and lived with his aunt and uncle until his marriage to Sarah Lord. He died in 1757 of smallpox.

Elizabeth and John had a happy marriage for 40 years before his death on Tortola Island, British Virgin Islands, in 1743. "I will venture to say few if any in the married state ever lived in sweeter harmony than we did," Elizabeth wrote in her memorial to John.

She continued to conduct plantation business activities after his death and donated land to be used by the Quakers to build the Haddonfield Monthly Meeting House. She served as a clerk of the women's meeting for 50 years, until her death at age 82 on March 30, 1762.

Elizabeth had inherited most of her father's property in the area when he died in 1724, and Ebenezar Hopkins' children inherited the property at Elizabeth's death.

In Haddonfield, in the Cemetery of the Friends Meeting, affixed to an old sycamore tree, is a bronze plaque that reads:

In Memory of
Elizabeth Haddon
Daughter of John Haddon of London
Wife of John Estaugh
She was Founder and Proprietor of
Haddonfield, New Jersey
Born 1680, Emigrated 1701
Married 1702, Died 1762
Originator of the Friends' Meeting
Here established in 1721
A Woman Remarkable for
Resolution Prudence Charity

Bibliography

Bacon, Margaret Hope. *Mothers of Feminism*. San Francisco: Harper & Row, 1986.

Longfellow, Henry Wadsworth. *The Works of Henry Wadsworth Longfellow*. Ware, England: Cumberland House, 1994.

McDonald, Gerald D. "Elizabeth Haddon Estaugh." In *Notable American Women 1607–1950*. Edward T. James, ed., vol. 1. Cambridge, Mass.: Harvard University Press, Belknap Press, 1971.

National Society of Colonial Dames of America. *A Few Unsung Women: Colonial and Pioneer*. Wendell, N.C.: Broadfoot, 1982.

12

Henrietta Deering Johnston

Henrietta Johnston was probably the first serious artist to come to live in the colonies. She was certainly the first woman to paint portraits in America.

Henrietta was born in Ireland, probably near Dublin, about 1680. It is thought she studied art with a church bishop named Simon Digby, at Elphin. Bishop Digby was recognized as a "greatmaster of painting in little watercolors." Sometime during her youth Henrietta learned a new pastel technique developed by Rosalba Carriera in Italy, possibly through lessons with artist Edward Lutterell, who painted in both London and Dublin.

Little else is known about Henrietta's early years except that her maiden name was Deering. She married Doctor Gideon Johnston in Dublin on April 11, 1705, after he had completed his studies at Trinity College. He planned to be a minister for the Anglican Church.

He was assigned a post as rector of the Saint Philip's Anglican Church in Charles Town (later Charleston) in South Carolina, and in 1707 the Johnstons left London with high hopes of making a good life in the New World, rearing a family and serving their fellow men and women in South Carolina at Saint Philip's.

With all the religious dissenters who had emigrated to the New World from England, the Anglican Church had to wage an uphill battle to keep any congregation in the colonies loyal to their denomination. New Englanders despised the official church so thoroughly, there would be no established Anglican churches there for years to come. The colonies of Virginia and South Carolina, however, were settled by Anglican members who, having come to the colonies for financial reasons rather than religious reform, wanted to remain a part of the church.

In 1701 the Society for the Propagation of the Gospel in Foreign Parts was organized by members of the Church of England in an attempt to bring religious teachings to native Americans and black people living in the colonies, as well as white people.

The Archbishop of Canterbury served as the first president of the society, which was also referred to as the Venerable Society.

The society enjoyed its greatest success in South Carolina, and the Church of England became a deep-rooted part of daily life of the settlers there. Ministers' salaries and expenses were paid from general taxes levied on all citizens of individual colonies, worshippers and dissenters alike. Some of the French Huguenots who had emigrated to South Carolina either joined the Anglican Church or supported the church officials in the South Carolina colony.

In addition to his post as rector, Gideon Johnston was also named to serve as Commissary to represent the Bishop of London in both Carolinas and the Bahamas.

Gideon's and Henrietta's hearts were filled with anticipation as the ship neared the coast of South Carolina. Two of Gideon's sons from his previous marriage accompanied them. When the ship docked at Madeira, Gideon went ashore to buy some provisions, and the ship sailed on without him! About six months went by before Gideon could secure passage on another ship bound for South Carolina. When he finally reached the port in Charles Town, he was so eager to see his family, he persuaded two other men to disembark with him and row in a small boat to shore before the ship docked.

It was an ill-fated move. One of his fellow passengers drowned during the attempt to reach the shore, and Gideon and the other adventurer were stranded almost two weeks on a small island offshore when their boat drifted because they had lost their oars.

Henrietta may have had second thoughts about her prospects with such a luckless husband, but, to quote Gideon from a letter he wrote later to relatives in England, "after sloops, perigoes and canoes were dispatched to all such places as it was thought we might be in ... a canoe got to us when we were at the last gasp and just upon the point of expiring, and next morning we were conveyed to the Port of the Continent where I lay a fortnight before I could recover strength enough to reach the town."

Gideon's bad luck had not ended. Because he took so long to reach South Carolina, the rectorship at St. Philip's Church had already been filled by a clergyman from the Maryland colony.

Henrietta and her stepsons had rented a house in the city since they could not live in the rectory before Gideon arrived. Charles Town was really a small village at the time, with only about 40 houses built inside the protective city walls and dirt paths that served as streets.

Henrietta had spent all the money she had brought with her, and for four months they existed on money Gideon borrowed from the Provincial treasury. Their rented home was burglarized on two different occasions, and several of their meager belongings were stolen. Gideon still suffered from his misadventure at sea, and Henrietta contracted malaria.

In September 1708, Gideon was finally installed as rector at St. Paul's Church in Colleton County, about 20 miles from Charles Town. The church building was not as fine as the one in Charles Town and the membership was not as distinguished. The church was constructed of brick, as was Saint Philip's, but it was smaller than most other churches in the area. The Johnston family, however, moved into the brick vicarage, with its garden, farmland stocked with cattle and a staff of two—a man and a woman.

By this time, however, Gideon had soured on the whole project.

He wrote a vituperative letter to his Bishop in London, complaining about his small salary and the general characters of the citizens of the New World at large and in Charles Town in particular. He wrote, "The people here ... are the vilest race of men upon the Earth; they have neither honor, nor honesty, nor religion.... New England, Pennsylvania, etc., are the most factious and seditious people in the whole world." Gideon's disgruntled self-pity was a handicap in his chosen profession, and Henrietta clearly had her work plain before her in dealing with a dissatisfied husband.

Henrietta had brought art supplies along when they had left England, and she went to work painting and drawing portraits of leading citizens in the Charles Town area to help pay her family's bills and debts.

In 1709 Gideon wrote an English friend, "Were it not for the assistance my wife gives me by drawing pictures ... I should not have been able to live."

Young James Johnston returned to England in 1710 to be educated, and money needs continued to increase.

Henrietta used colored chalk for the portraits she drew during this period. The portraits were of aristocratic French Huguenot settlers who had emigrated to South Carolina a few years earlier. She drew at least 40 such portraits.

The French Huguenots were the only group of settlers to escape Gideon's scathing condemnation. They were among the more prominent and better educated people in South Carolina. Dr. Francis LeJau, one of the French Huguenot ministers of the Anglican church of Saint James at Goose Creek, was a former classmate of Gideon's at Trinity College years before. Dr. LeJau had been highly successful in his ministry, and his church had enjoyed a steady growth in membership. He had started a mission school for black and Indian children as a part of his missionary efforts. Dr. LeJau's outstanding success may have contributed to Gideon's dissatisfaction with his own location.

Art was much more than a pleasant hobby for a bored housewife in Henrietta's life. She used both men and women as her subjects, one portrait being of Colonel William Rhett, who fought fiercely against pirates attempting to rob ships sailing in and out of Charles Town harbor.

Henrietta's half-length portraits of Charles Town women were graceful and elegant, but she never included the subject's hands in the portrait. She found hands difficult to paint.

By 1711 Henrietta decided to return to England to get more art supplies. She was asked to carry to church officials in London petitions from local clergymen requesting more money for their work in the colonies.

Henrietta hoped the ocean voyage would help improve her health, which had been deteriorating since the births of her two daughters. Gideon was not allowed to go with his family because of his heavy indebtedness. According to colonial law, debtors could not leave the colony. He even had to borrow the money to pay passages for Henrietta and his children.

Henrietta, her two daughters and stepson, Robert, left port at Charles Town in April 1711, and by November of that year, Gideon was complaining bitterly to her in letters about conditions in Charles Town. He wrote, "Instead of ... fluttering of people up and down the streets, very few are seen to walk abroad, and there is scarce anything to be heard but sighs and complaints, and sad accents of sorrow at every corner."

To the Society for the Propagation of the Gospel in Foreign Parts, Gideon wrote, "Never was there a more sickly or fatal season than this for smallpox, pestilential fevers, pleurisies.... Three funerals of a day, and sometimes four are now very usual; and all I get by these is a few rotten gloves and an abundance of trouble day and night...." The giving of pairs of gloves at funeral services was a prevalent custom of the time, and they were presented to guests at funerals as well as to the presiding minister.

By March 1712, Gideon wrote the society he had become both lame and blind. Could he return to England?

It took a year to convince the society to allow Gideon to return. While he was on a ship sailing back to England in March 1713, he passed Henrietta and their two daughters on another ship returning to South Carolina.

In 1714 a severe hurricane badly damaged Saint Paul's Church, which had never been completely finished. Henrietta kindly allowed storm victims who had lost their homes and the pitiful homeless victims of a recent local Indian uprising, whose homes had been burned, to move into the vicarage to live for a time.

While Gideon was still in England, Henrietta continued to follow her artistic endeavors faithfully. Her portraits were now more often watercolors or crayon drawings.

Gideon was in no hurry to return to Charles Town, with the ever-present threat of piracy on the high seas. It was 1715 before he returned, and was in no better mood than before he left and was soon wishing he could get back to England, where his two sons were being educated.

To add to his distress, the house in which the Johnstons had lived on the church property was badly damaged during the Indian attack and would require extensive repairs and all the out-buildings had been burned.

Gideon never got back to England. In April 1716, he was escorting Governor Craven to a ship in the Charles Town harbor, when his sloop capsized in heavy seas. Gideon was too weak to get off the vessel and swim to shore by himself, so he drowned.

Henrietta was left with no money and only her artistic talent with which to support her two daughters and a niece who had joined the family a few months before.

In 1725 Henrietta took her family to New York, where she painted several portraits for wealthy citizens before moving back to Charles Town in 1727. After their return they attended Saint Philip's Church.

Henrietta died sometime in 1728, according to the register in St. Philip's, and she was buried on March 7 that year. Only her art remains to prove that she lived. A collection of her portraits were shown in the *Smithsonian Magazine* of February 1978.

Bibliography

Colonial Dames of America. *A Few Unsung Women: Colonial and Pioneer.* Wendell, N.C.: Broadfoot, 1982.

Hirsch, Arthur Henry. *The Huguenots of Colonial South Carolina.* Durham, N.C.: Duke University Press, 1928.

Weir, Robert M. *Colonial South Carolina: A History.* Millwood, N.Y.: KTO, 1983.

13

Susanna Wright

Susanna Wright was a colonial woman ahead of her time. She worked willingly doing the usual household tasks for her parents and various siblings, but she also found time to serve her colony in an official capacity as prothonotary, to cultivate silkworms and to write poetry.

Susanna was born the first of eight children, in Warrington, Lancashire, England, on August 4, 1697, to John and Patience Gibson Wright. The Wrights were of the Quaker faith and they came to America primarily to try to earn more money to support their family and live among fellow Quakers.

John Wright had studied medicine in England, but he believed he should devote a portion of his time to his Quaker ministry, and the practice of medicine did not allow him to do this. He became a bodice maker in England, but that was not profitable enough, and he decided to emigrate with his family to the New World and join the colony of Pennsylvania, established by his good friend William Penn. Young Susanna remained in England to complete her education.

The Wright family arrived in Pennsylvania in June 1714, and settled in the Chester County area where Mr. Wright opened a tailor shop on the banks of the Susquehanna River. His new venture was not profitable, and in 1726 he bought land in Lancaster County, where he and two of his sons started another business. To cross the river a private boat had to be hired, and so the Wrights began the operation of a ferry service in 1727 on the Susquehanna. The ferry was composed of two canoes joined together with lashings, but it furnished entry into the Great Valley on the frontier.

Susanna completed her education and joined her family only a few months before her mother died in 1722. For the next 20 years, Susanna served as a substitute mother for her younger brothers and sisters in their family home of Hempfield. She was extremely busy as her father was away from home frequently.

Samuel Blunston owned property adjoining the Wright homestead, and he became attracted to young Susanna. After a romance of a few months, a misunderstanding arose between the couple, and they ended their romance. Subsequently, Mr. Blunston married a wealthy widow named Mrs. Bilton.

Susanna must have been disappointed by the turn of events, but she and her family remained on friendly terms with both Mr. and Mrs. Blunston.

In time, John Wright became active in the community government and served as a local judge for several years. Later both he and Blunston were members of the Provincial Assembly.

Since the Wright ferry landing was at Hempfield, Susanna was unofficial hostess for all visitors to the area. She became friends with Benjamin Franklin and his wife, Deborah, Isaac and Charles Norris, James Logan, and other noted Pennsylvania residents, as well as Quakers. There was a Meeting House at Wrights's Ferry.

Benjamin Franklin was so impressed by Susanna's common sense, he took her advice on how best to obtain horses for General Braddock and his men. Franklin wrote Susanna: "I thought from the first that your proposal of calling several Townships together was very judicious. I was only at a Loss how to get them called by some appearance of Authority. On the Road from your Place hither, I considered that at the Court of Oyer and Terminer here, there would probably be constables from most of the Townships, and if the Chief Justice could be prevailed on to recommend it from the Bench ... perhaps the business might by that means be effectually done...." Susanna's judgment must have been highly regarded for Benjamin Franklin to heed her advice!

Susanna and her family were popular members of the Quaker society. In 1755 Sally Armitt in Philadelphia wrote Susanna: "It is impossible to express the uneasiness that I am under on account of your Family, I wish you would come to town, as it must be more dangerous on the river, dear Susy — We have Several Spare rooms which you shall be very welcome to and we shall take it as a favour. I know Thee would not chuse to be in a Family where Thee could not make free, dear Susy, Thee shall be as if at home in our House." Armitt feared an Indian attack on the Wright family as the Mohawk Indian tribe had been joining with British armed forces, then engaged in battles with French soldiers for control of Canadian territory. England's government believed the colonists should provide men and financing for the struggle, but the colonists had little enthusiasm for it.

In a letter dated April 18, 1755, from one member of the Assembly of 1755 to his relative, the member wrote, "The ancient King of the Mohawks ... came down with some of his warriors this Winter to Philadelphia, and assured them of his friendship, though he owned [admitted] many of the young Mohawks were gone over to the Enemy...."

William Penn had always believed his colony would be safe from the Indians so long as they were well treated, and he made no provisions for his settlers' defense. After Penn died in 1718, nothing was changed, and the colonists still had no way to defend themselves.

As settlers moved farther inland, however, occasional Indian massacres occurred, and the Scotch-Irish and German farmers demanded some kind of effort be made by the Pennsylvania colony government to protect them and their families.

Patriot Benjamin Franklin, a Boston citizen who had moved to Pennsylvania, told the officials in August 1756 that the settlers did need help: "Our frontier people are continually butchered.... I do not believe we shall ever have a firm peace with the Indians till we have well drubbed them."

Quaker supporters still living in England were also alarmed by the dreadful Indian attacks, and they urged the pacifists in the Pennsylvania government to resign before the colony was destroyed. Most of them did resign that same year, and the new government, composed of non–Quakers, declared war on the Indians, and the colony was saved from annihilation.

In her later years Susanna raised silkworms as something of a hobby, although the culture of the worms was tedious and required close attention. She reeled the silk produced in the cocoons and won a £10 prize in 1771 for having the most silkworms raised by one person.

Historian Robert Proud said he heard Susanna say her 1,500 silkworms could grow to a colony numbering 1,000,000 if she gave it more time and effort. The manufacture of linen was also encouraged by the Pennsylvania government, but Susanna left that to other women and concentrated on silk.

Susanna dyed the silk thread she harvested with her own homemade dyes, but she sent the thread to England to be woven into cloth. At one time, she received 60 yards of mantua silk back from an English weaving company. A court dress made from her silk was given to Queen Charlotte by Benjamin Franklin, and the Queen sent Susanna a beautiful portfolio in return.

Susanna came to be considered something of an expert in the manufacture and dying of the silk fabric that she and some of the other women colonists made, as is evidenced in a letter to her from Mrs. Robert Moore in 1771: "I took the opportunity of sending some samples of ... my attempts ... in the art of dyeing.... The scarlet ... and the Purple are both dyed with Brazilleto Salt Tartar and Alum....

The yellow is dyed with Barberry root which I boiled ... with a little Allum and [I] was much pleased with the colour it produced...."

Samuel Blunston's wife died, and his health failed. Susanna still felt affection for him, and she managed all his business affairs for several years before his death. In 1745 Blunston bequeathed her 900 acres of land and the house in which he lived. She would own the property for her lifetime.

Blunston had been the prothonotary, or chief official in the district, who could certify legal documents such as deeds, take sworn statements from witnesses unable to attend Court sessions and take affidavits. After his death, Susanna was commissioned prothonotary, which was again an affirmation of her capabilities in business.

Susanna and her brother James and his family moved to Blunston's house to live after the Blunston estate was settled in 1745. There Susanna had more space for her large library, and from her new location she conducted her community activities, as well as supervised the rearing of James's children. She was required to settle frequent disputes between the colonists and local Indians concerning land rights and ownership, pasturing rights for cattle, and other such legal matters. She was a good friend to the Conestoga Indians.

She also distilled herbal remedies for relatives and neighbors, based on her own studies and the medical information passed on to her from her father.

Deborah Norris Logan, daughter of family friend Charles Norris, wrote in a letter to a friend, describing Susanna Wright in her later years: "She was small in person and had never been handsome, but had a penetrating, sensible countenance, and was truly polite and courteous.... She was well acquainted with books.... She spoke and wrote French with great ease and fluency. She had a knowledge of Latin and could read Italian and had made considerable attainment in many of the sciences."

Also Susanna wrote poetry of the sad "graveyard" type, common for that day and age, and some of her poems in manuscript form can be seen at the Library Company of Philadelphia. A piece of silk cloth made from the production of silk harvested by Susanna is on display at the same location.

Susanna did not take any of her silk for her own use. She dressed in the plain drab tan and brown calico clothing favored by Quaker female believers.

Susanna died on December 1, 1784, at 87 years of age. She was buried in the Quaker cemetery at Columbia, but no stone marks her grave. Quakers did not have a custom of grave markers.

Mr. Blunston's niece inherited his property at Susanna's death, and James Wright built a large home of his own in Columbia.

Bibliography

Bacon, Margaret Hope. *Mothers of Feminism*. San Francisco: Harper & Row, 1986.

Faris, John T. *The Romance of Old Philadelphia*. Philadelphia: J.B. Lippincott, 1918.

Neidle, Cecyle S. *America's Immigrant Women*. New York: Hippocrene Books, 1975.

14

Marie Madeleine Hachard

Madeleine Hachard was an 18-year-old novice nun when she first came to the New Orleans colony in the Louisiana Territory in August 1726 from Rouen, France. She was a member of the Ursuline Order, a teaching order of nuns of Roman Catholic faith.

Madeleine's friends and relatives cried when she was preparing to leave them, and one of her brothers objected so fiercely that he and Madeleine were estranged for a time.

Madeleine's parents had seen four of their children enter the religious life, and they felt Madeleine too deserved her chance to follow her heart.

Actually the petite young woman, not quite five feet in height, dreaded leaving her home, her family and France, but she bravely assured everyone she would be fine.

She and her six nun companions first rode many miles by stagecoach across France as crowds along the way waved and cheered. Later their carriage got mired in muddy ruts in the road they traveled, and the young women were forced to seek shelter with an elderly woman who lived along the road.

When at last they approached the ship, the *Gironde*, which would carry them to the New World, Madeleine admitted her misgivings in a letter she wrote to her parents.

"It is only God, whose voice I hear and follow, who could separate me from parents whose tender love I have a thousand times felt," she assured them.

The ship had barely left the dock when it struck a rock. The Ursulines were terrified that the ship would sink, but it did not. Later a violent storm rose with wild wind that significantly slowed their progress and forced the girls to tie themselves to their bunks to prevent being injured as the ship tossed and plunged in the heavy seas. A priest was on board also, and he calmed them. Then the sea was calm for weeks while the nuns prayed and the sailors roared and raved. When the ship finally reached the Gulf of Mexico, it ran aground on a sandbank.

The ship's crew was forced to throw cargo and supplies for the Ursulines' mission overboard. At last the ship floated free, and they moved toward the mouth of the Mississippi River.

Madeleine wrote letters back to her father in France, indicating she and her companions were appalled by the sights they saw in the Louisiana swamps. For five days they traveled by boat upriver to the town of New Orleans through a subtropical environment inhabited by alligators, snakes and other wild creatures, none of which the girls had ever seen before. Beautiful blue- and coral-colored birds flashed through the air, and the whole landscape appeared to be in constant motion.

Each night they camped along the way, the mosquitoes moved in swarms at sunset, and the crew fought the insects for the rest of the night as the Sisters tried to sleep.

For the French women, the entire experience must have seemed like a nightmare, and their eventual arrival in New Orleans must have come as a relief, although they saw it was little more than a large village.

Madeleine and her sisters had work to do, however, and they started working willingly. Their assigned tasks included caring for, protecting and educating young girls of marriageable age who had been sent to the area by the king of France to be wives of French soldiers on duty in the Louisiana colony, still under control of the French government. For the next 20 years they worked with new girls sent each year.

The king's girls were furnished with a small trunk or chest (*cassette* in French) that was filled with clothes for their trousseaus and some linens for use in their new homes. These young women were called *les filles à la cassette* or Casket Girls. Most married quickly and left the protection of the nuns.

In 1706 King Louis XIV of France had sent 20 young women from respectable family backgrounds to serve as companions or wives for his soldiers. There were no Sisters in the area at that time, and none of the girls was impressed with Louisiana. They did not like eating Indian corn, so prominent in the local diet, and were generally displeased with conditions, so they staged a petticoat rebellion and went back home to France.

Many citizens of the Acadian province in Canada had emigrated to Louisiana when England took control of Canada, and they were glad to have the Ursuline Sisters join them.

The Sisters found poverty, homeless people and many orphaned children, for whom the nuns provided care and education. The Ursulines founded the oldest multiracial school for both sexes in the colonies. The school run by the nuns was open to all children in New Orleans, including American Indians and the children of slaves.

The nuns were given duties in the hospital that was already there, and they worked to improve the quality of care, all of which kept Madeleine and the other Sisters busy. The priest found a church already built also.

Madeleine adjusted well to her new surroundings, but she could not agree that New Orleans rivaled Paris, as had been alleged by other settlers of the area. In time, perhaps, but not yet.

When Madeleine arrived, levees were being constructed to protect New Orleans from the inevitable flooding that occurred during rainy seasons. With the elevation of New Orleans being only one foot above the average level of the water in the Gulf of Mexico, homes were flooded annually.

The government officials in Louisiana were glad to have the nuns join their community, and they built a convent for them. Since the officials had frequent sharp disagreements among themselves, when the building was completed it was too small and was already undergoing deterioration caused by the delay of several months in getting a roof installed on the wooden building. Unfortunately, rain continued falling during the delay.

While the convent was being built, Madeleine and her companions lived in a house formerly owned by an aristocrat located on the corner of Chartres and Bienville streets.

In 1721 the French King sent a group of 80 girls from the Paris houses of correction to become his lonely soldiers' brides, but they were deemed unattractive and Governor Bienville, the colonial governor of Louisiana, protested that his officers could manage to find husbands for only two of the girls, and the others would probably stay unmarried. Even the soldiers protested about the lack of beauty and grace of the prospective brides. They said they would be willing to settle for more beauty and less virtue!

Madeleine reassured her parents repeatedly that she was in no way suffering in her new location. She wrote, "There is as much of magnificence and politeness as in France.... Cloth of gold and velours are commonplace here, albeit three times dearer than at Rouen."

She told them food was plentiful, but high in cost. "We eat here meat, fish, peas, wild peppers, and many fruits and vegetables, such as bananas which are the most excellent of all fruits. In a word we live on buffalo, lamb, swans, wild geese and wild turkeys, rabbits, chickens, ducks, pheasant, doves, quail and other birds and game of different species.... They use here much chocolate with milk and coffee."

She was especially impressed by the wonderful taste of Louisiana yams, or sweet potatoes, when they were cooked "in the ashes like chestnuts."

She was homesick sometimes, as when she complained she was "much nearer the sun than at Rouen" when the weather was hot and sultry. The mosquitoes continued to plague her, and she said, "Sometimes they are in such great number that one may cut them with a knife!"

The elaborate dresses and finery worn by the women in New Orleans irritated her sense of fitness. She wrote, "The women here as elsewhere employ powder and rouge to conceal the wrinkles in their faces; indeed, the demon here possesses a great empire, but that merely strengthens our hope of destroying it."

Madeleine was not being unduly critical of the New Orleans women. A French soldier stationed in New Orleans in 1743 wrote his family that the rich people spent their time watching their slaves work to clear and improve the land while they spent the money they received from crops grown on the land "on plays, balls and feasts, but the most common pastime of the highest as well as the lowest, and even of the slaves is gambling," confirming Madeleine's own statements.

The celebration of Mardi Gras was established from the beginning of colonization in Louisiana, and included feasting, imbibing alcoholic beverages and general revelry in the period before Lent began.

The Ursuline nuns inadvertently started the world famous Mardi Gras parade in 1734. By that time the convent had been replaced by a new building and at last it was moving day for the Sisters and their young charges, the orphaned children in their care. The nuns dressed the children as angels and marched along with them, followed by priests, soldiers and citizens helping move their belongings to the new convent. All stepped along to lively music as colonial Governor Bienville watched with approval.

The children loved it, and there was little cost involved, so the nuns decided to make a little parade an annual event of the Lenten season.

From that humble beginning the parade underwent many changes to become the spectacle it is today, with about 500,000 spectators lining the streets of New Orleans to watch the many parades included in the present-day Mardi Gras festival. While the parade began as a religious event, it evolved into a festival sponsored by municipal officials and attracts many visitors to New Orleans.

The Sisters never left their assigned duties. In times of hurricanes, they prayed with other residents. During the terrible epidemics of various lowland fevers, they nursed and comforted stricken citizens.

Madeleine served her Order for 35 years, and she never returned to France or her family. She always gave her work her best effort, as the convent records show.

In early August 1760, Madeleine did not attend Mass. When one of the other nuns went to see about her, they found Madeleine had died in her sleep. Her work was finished.

Bibliography

Chitwood, Oliver Perry. *History of Colonial America*. New York: Harper Brothers, 1931.
Kane, Harnett T. *Queen New Orleans*. New York: William Morrow, 1949.
Martin, James Kirby, et al. *America and Its People*. New York: Harper Collins, 1989.

15

Elizabeth Timothy

When the Edict of Nantes, which had promised religious freedom to French citizens, was repealed in France in 1685, and King Louis XIV tried to force French citizens to adopt the state religion, he brought about the same results as the English king and Parliament had many years before — there was a mass exodus out of France.

These fleeing French Huguenots went to various European countries for refuge, and some came directly to colonies in North America.

In 1629 King Charles I granted Sir Robert Heath a huge amount of property which covered the area from the Virginia boundary to Spanish Florida. Heath negotiated with the Huguenots about colonizing the "Carolana" region, and plans were made to have salt works established there. The Huguenots also hoped to make "Carolana" a religious refuge for their sect to believers.

Louis Timothee's father was one of the Huguenots who left France. He went to Holland where he settled and reared his family. Young Louis learned to be a printer. While he was learning his trade, Louis met his future wife, Elizabeth.

Elizabeth's maiden name is unknown, but she was born, reared and educated in Holland, where she was taught accounting business methods. They were married about 1722.

Feeling the New World offered better opportunities for financial advancement, Louis, Elizabeth and their four children emigrated to Philadelphia, in the Pennsylvania colony, from Rotterdam on September 21, 1731.

Louis got a job as a printer with patriot Benjamin Franklin, and the Timothee family lived in Philadelphia for about two years. Louis was the first librarian of the Philadelphia Library Company.

There were few printers in the colonies at the time, and even though the Ruling Assembly in South Carolina offered a bounty for a printer to locate in their colony in 1722, it was about three years before a printer named Thomas Whitmarsh accepted the £1,000 offered by the Assembly and opened a print and publishing shop in South Carolina.

After Mr. Whitmarsh died in 1733, Louis and Elizabeth Timothee decided to move their family to live in Charles Town, South Carolina, to take advantage of the opportunities there. With the financial assistance of Franklin, Louis Timothee bought the *South Carolina Gazette* from the estate of Whitmarsh.

In February 1734, Louis anglicized his name to Lewis Timothy, and revived the *Gazette* on Church Street. The printing office also served an an unofficial post office and distribution center for letters and packages.

Elizabeth Timothy had been busy in these early years with the births and rearing of six children, but when her husband was tragically killed in an accident, Elizabeth was forced to assume operation of the publishing and printing enterprise. It was a difficult decision for her to make as she was in the last weeks of her seventh pregnancy.

Elizabeth began her publishing career with the following open letter to subscribers:

> Whereas the late Printer of this Gazette hath been deprived of his life by an Unhappy Accident, I take this opportunity of informing the Publick, that I shall continue the said Paper; and hope, by the Assistance of my Friends to make it entertaining and correct as may be reasonably expected....

With this announcement, Elizabeth Timothy became one of the first female newspaper publishers in any of the colonies and one of the first women journalists in the world.

In her announcement, she added she hoped the subscribers and other readers would "be kindly pleased to continue their favors and good offices to his poor afflicted widow, and six small children, and another hourly expected." Her activities or some health problem may have caused the premature birth of the baby; there is no later mention of the child in accounts of her life.

Lewis had published the *Gazette* once a week, but Elizabeth published the paper every Monday and Thursday from 1738 to 1746, in her son Peter's name. Peter was now 14 years old and he helped his mother in the business. The newspaper was always published on time.

Colonial printers were not essayists or writers in the usual sense of the word. They were essentially printers of what news they could uncover, providing the details of legislative actions taken by the Assembly and serving as printers of government documents.

There was little demand for books to be printed in the colonies as these were imported from Europe, so few printers printed anything larger than pamphlets.

Elizabeth was very successful, both as a publisher and as a mother. Her paper thrived during the six years she was in charge, while she also collected debts and took care of her children, including the newest baby. Sadly two of her sons died in 1739 from one of the fevers so common in the lowlands.

Elizabeth was not afraid to print controversial material. She printed religious articles by the Reverend George Whitefield of Ireland, who held popular but inflammatory opinions, and who was a friend of her son, Peter Timothy. Peter stood trial with the Reverend Whitefield in South Carolina when they were charged with libeling local ministers.

She included articles in her newspaper about the harsh treatment and punishment of slaves in South Carolina.

She published inoculation stories during the town's 1739 yellow fever epidemic, which claimed the lives of her own two sons, and she supported Eliza Lucas in her indigo project with an article entitled "Instructions on the Cultivation of Indigo."

Elizabeth's articles were reprinted by Benjamin Franklin in Philadelphia, and in England the *Gentlemen's Magazine* depended on Elizabeth's newspapers as its own most reliable source of news from the colonies.

Lewis Timothy had been somewhat dilatory in making payments to Franklin, but Franklin went on to say that Elizabeth, as the manager, "continued to account with the greatest regularity and exactitude every quarter afterwards and managed the business with such success that she not only brought up a ... family of children, but at the expiration of the term [of the partnership agreement between Franklin and Lewis Timothy] was able to purchase of me the printing house and establish her son in it."

Peter Timothy assumed full control of the printing establishment at age 21 in 1746. Elizabeth operated a stationery and book store, while she continued to juggle her duties as a mother and grandmother with shopkeeping.

Peter Timothy was very active in local government affairs, and in 1776 he served as secretary of the Constitutional Congress, which wrote the South Carolina State Constitution. He was one of the founders of the library in Charles Town in 1743, and belonged to the Charles Town Library Society, established in 1748.

Peter Timothy married Ann Donovan on December 8, 1745, in Charles Town, about the same time he assumed control of the newspaper. They would have a large family, about 15 children, only eight of which would survive infancy.

After Benjamin Franklin invented the lightning rod, Peter urged his readers to try it to prevent lightning damage to their homes and other buildings. He named his son Benjamin Franklin Timothy, and kept Franklin informed about the young boy's progress.

Charles Town citizens who owned plantations were wealthy, and they enjoyed some of life's finer pleasures, such as theater and music. A theater was built about 1725, where visiting actors presented plays. There were public musical offerings by the time the Timothy family came to live in the area, and regular concerts were presented after 1762 by the Saint Cecilia Society.

In 1773 the first museum in North America was started. Sadly the library, with its 6,000 books, burned completely in 1776.

Elizabeth Timothy died in 1757. The inventory of personal effects listed two French Bibles, a "parcel of books," a marble-covered sideboard, two old desks and a few other pieces of furniture in her estate. In addition she left six small items of jewelry, 38 ounces of old silver, some pewter articles, a few pieces of china and some fireplace tools.

The total value was about £25 in currency. There were still a number of outstanding debts she had never been able to collect that had been owed to Lewis.

Elizabeth also left to her heirs a large tract of land with three houses and eight slaves. Obviously she had profited from her career as a newspaper printer and editor.

In addition to her son Peter, three daughters survived Elizabeth: Louisa, who married James Richards; Mary Elizabeth, who married Abraham Bowquin; and Catherine, who married Theodore Trezevant.

In 1781 when the Revolutionary War brought British Armed Forces to Charles Town and they occupied the city for several months, Peter suspended publication of the newspaper and moved his family to Philadelphia.

The next year Peter and two of his daughters sailed to Santo Domingo in an effort to get funds to reopen the newspaper business in South Carolina, but they all died when the ship on which they were passengers sank in stormy seas.

Ann Timothy, Peter's wife, went back to Charles Town in 1782, and on July 16, 1783, following the example of her beloved mother-in-law, she resumed publication of the newspaper, which she renamed *Gazette of the State of South Carolina*. She continued publication until her death in 1792. Ann was also named printer to the State during her career and printed official government documents.

Charles Town was incorporated and renamed Charleston in 1792 also.

Benjamin Franklin Timothy, Ann and Peter's son, inherited the newspaper from his mother. He continually published it until 1802, when he retired. He died in 1807.

Benjamin Franklin Timothy's nephew inherited his uncle's printing business, and he later merged it with the *Charleston Courier*. The newspaper is now published under the name of the *Charleston News and Courier*.

Bibliography

Brown, Richard Maxwell. *Notable American Women*. Vol. 4. Cambridge, Mass.: Harvard University Press, Belknap Press, 1971.

Hirsch, Arthur Henry. *The Huguenots of Colonial South Carolina*. Durham, N.C.: Duke University Press, 1928.

Weir, Robert M. *Colonial South Carolina: A History*. Millwood, N.J.: Kraus-Thomson, 1983.

16

Eliza Lucas Pinckney

Although Eliza Lucas was born in Antiqua in the West Indies, she was educated in England, where she developed an intense lifelong interest in plants and agriculture. Her father, Colonel George Lucas, encouraged her in her agricultural pursuits. He was a member of the British Armed Forces in Antiqua and had little time to indulge his own similar interests in experimental agriculture.

About the time Eliza finished her education, Colonel Lucas decided to move his family to one of the new colonies recently settled on the North American continent. A large number of people from Barbados, Antiqua and other West Indian towns had already gone to colonies in the New World, settling largely in the Carolina colony.

Colonel Lucas had inherited three plantations in the South Carolina colony from his father, John Lucas. The one Colonel Lucas chose for his homestead was a 600-acre tract on Wappoo Creek, not far up the Ashley River, 17 land miles from Charleston. His other two properties comprised a 2,950-acre plantation on the Waccamaw River and a 1,500-acre plantation on the Combahee River.

Colonel Lucas brought his family to South Carolina in 1738. Eliza was 16 years old, but her little sister, Polly, was only three. Two of Eliza's brothers were attending school in England.

Eliza's mother was an invalid, which left Eliza in charge of household activities. Soon Eliza learned she would also be expected to oversee plantation activities when her father had to return to Antiqua. Colonel Lucas felt his daughter was competent to manage his business affairs in South Carolina. She assured him she loved "the vegitable world extremely."

Colonel Lucas had living quarters and outbuildings erected on the plantation before he returned to military duty in Antiqua. He bought slaves to help Eliza do the heavy work, and he told her it would be her responsibility to conduct various agricultural experiments for him.

Colonel Lucas's faith in Eliza was well founded. When he sent her seeds of plants not grown in South Carolina or a few plants of a new variety, Eliza planted and tended them faithfully to see if they could be developed into a profitable crop.

An entry in her journal dated July 1739 says, "I wrote my father a very long letter on his plantation affairs ... on the pains I had taken to bring the Indigo, Ginger, Cotton, Lucern, and Cassada to perfection, and had greater hopes from the Indigo ... if I could have the seeds earlier next year from the West Indies, than any of ye rest of ye things I had tryed ... also concerning pitch and tar and lime and other plantation affairs." In her letter Eliza also asked her father to advise her on different aspects of planting, such as the best types of soil to use.

Some of the plants adapted well to the South Carolina climate, while others would not grow or would not mature. It was through the cultivation of the indigo plant that Eliza enjoyed her greatest success. The indigo plant was a source of blue dye used in dying textiles, which were manufactured in many countries, and it would have a ready-made market.

Eliza had to make sure the soil was properly prepared before the seeds were planted, and the plants required close attention as they grew. When ready for harvest, the leaves were stripped from the plants and soaked in vats for days. When the leaves had fermented and attained a deep blue color, the liquid, which became the dye itself, was drained into another vat. Here the dye was beaten until it thickened, after which it was allowed to settle for a few days. The third step involved removing the clear liquid remaining on top, leaving only the heavy blue sediment at the bottom of the container. The sediment was then removed and allowed to dry in the hot sun. After it dried and hardened, the indigo was cut into large cubes to be sold for dying purposes.

Colonel Lucas sent a man from the West Indies to work for Eliza as overseer of the plantation, but the overseer, either incompetent or fearing the dye from the Lucas plantation would cut into West Indies indigo markets, produced bad dye. Eliza had to ask him to leave when she found out he had ruined a large amount of dye.

Colonel Lucas then hired a French Huguenot, Andrew Deveraux, to assist Eliza, and with the help of this new man, Eliza was able to produce a marketable product, but in small amounts.

Life was not all work for Eliza. When Mrs. Boddicott, a family friend in England with whom Eliza had boarded during her school years, became concerned about Eliza's heavy responsibilities and isolated life, Eliza hastened to reassure her friend that she was active socially.

In a letter to Mrs. Boddicott, Eliza wrote, "I like this part of the world.... We have a very good acquaintance from which we have received much friendship and civility. Charles Town, the principal [town] in this province is a polite agreeable place, the people live very genteel and very much in the English taste."

Apparently Colonel Lucas also became concerned about Eliza's social life, or lack thereof. She reported to him that she enjoyed "a very genteel entertainment and ball" on a visit to Charles Town in 1742. The ball was given by the colonial governor to honor the king's birthday. Eliza mentioned that she had danced with an old friend of her father's, who was now living in the area.

Eliza enjoyed gaiety, but more than balls and house parties she enjoyed quieter pursuits. She loved reading, practicing music on her pianoforte, writing letters and taking walks through plantation fields. She always visited a close friend and neighbor named Mrs. Chardon on Tuesdays, and other friends on Fridays.

Due to the continued invalidism of her mother, Anne Lucas, Eliza had the complete responsibility of seeing that servants performed their daily household tasks properly. Also Eliza tutored her little sister and two black girls living on the plantation in basic educational subjects. On Thursdays she paid bills and conducted other plantation business as needed.

But Eliza's true passions remained plants and agriculture. She planted a large grove of oaks to supply future shipbuilders she felt sure would eventually come to South Carolina. She set out fig trees in an orchard, planning to dry the harvest from them and export the fruit. Her friends teased her about her "fertile brain at scheming," but they were truly fascinated by Eliza's wide-ranging activities and never-ending projects.

During her teen years Eliza formed a closed friendship with another girl named Mary Bartlett, whose Uncle Charles Pinckney loaned Eliza his copies of Plutarch and Virgil to read in her spare time. He and his wife, who was in poor health, often invited the two girls to have tea with them, for Mary was a favorite niece.

As Eliza matured into a young woman, her father realized she would probably want to marry and have a family. He began to consider suitable prospects and wrote to ask her opinion of two men, either of whom, he felt, would be a suitable husband for her.

Eliza replied, "[I hope] that a single life is not my only choice and if it were not as I am yet but eighteen, hope you will [put] aside the thoughts of my marrying yet these two or three years at least."

She thanked him for his interest in her future and paternal "tenderness," but she told him she did not consider either of his choices appealing. One of the men was rich but much older than she, and she felt she could not "form sentiments favorable enough" to marry him. As she was only slightly acquainted with the younger suitor mentioned by her father, she had no opinion of him.

Eliza begged her father to allow her a few more years at home and told him, "You are so good to say you have too great an opinion of my prudence to think I would entertain an indiscreet passion for anyone, and I hope Heaven will direct me that I may never disappoint you.... I am certain I would indulge no passion that had not your approbation."

By 1744 Eliza had demonstrated to her own satisfaction that large profits could be made from growing crops of indigo. She used the entire crop that year to furnish seeds to her neighboring planters. Within three years the neighbors and Eliza were harvesting enough indigo to export it to other countries, especially those in Europe.

By 1754 South Carolina planters exported 10,000 pounds of indigo dye cakes, which was a valuable addition to the local economy. It took 100 pounds of rice to buy one pound of indigo! Indigo remained a major cash crop in South Carolina until the Revolutionary War.

Eliza's friend, Mrs. Pinckney, died in 1743, and Eliza's mother and little sister returned to Antiqua. Eliza's brothers had to leave their school in England and return to Antiqua because of illness.

The next year Eliza launched a new project — matrimony. Her choice was her own, and it was the recently widowed Colonel Pinckney. He was more than twice Eliza's age of 21, but this time age did not appear to be a barrier to romance. He was a member of the aristocracy of South Carolina and well respected, so Eliza's parents approved her choice, and the two were married on May 27, 1744.

The Pinckney plantation was located about five miles outside Charles Town and was called Belmont. Belmont became Eliza's new home, and she left the care of her father's other plantation in the hands of his overseer.

The Pinckneys had four children born during their marriage: a son, Charles Cotesworth, was born in 1746; a daughter, Harriott, was born in 1748; and a second son, Thomas, was born in 1750. Son George Lucas was born in 1747, but he died five days later.

Eliza devoted her time and attention to her children with the same intensity she had shown earlier with agricultural pursuits. When Charles, her first child, was not yet a year old, she wrote to ask a friend in England to send her a special toy, "a description of which I enclose, to teach him according to Mr. Lock's method (which I have carefully studied) to play himself into learning."

Colonel Pickney was also apparently a devoted father, as he made little Charles some toys to teach him his alphabet, although the little boy was not yet even talking.

The next year Eliza wrote her English friend proudly that "little Charles can tell all his letters in any book without hesitation and begins to spell before he is two years old!"

Even with motherhood now a factor in her life, Eliza still supervised her father's plantation overseer, and she tried a new venture of cultivating silkworms and making silk.

In 1752 she sent to China for silkworm eggs. When they arrived, Eliza carefully supervised the drying of the cocoons. She had plantation children pulling leaves from the mulberry trees native to South Carolina to feed the larvae. As the worms matured and spun the silk thread, Eliza and some of her women servants wound the thread on reels. They harvested enough raw silk to make three women's dresses.

The next year, when Eliza, her husband and her three children went to England, she took the dresses with her. When Eliza was presented to the British royal family, she wore one of the dresses made from her silkworm thread. The English people were impressed by the beauty of the silk and hoped much more could be produced in the Carolina colonies.

Colonel Pinckney's reason for going to England was to be a commissioner for the Charles Town colony, and he knew his business affairs would require his presence in England for several months, or possibly years. Because they did not want to be apart for such a long period of time, his family went with him.

The Pinckneys traveled throughout England, visiting friends and relatives, covering some 700 miles in all. After visiting the resort city of Bath, they returned to London to live in the furnished house they rented there.

Eliza enjoyed attending the London theatres and various social gatherings to which they were invited, but she was surprised by the enormous amount of time many of the society women spent playing card games. The games were played for extremely high stakes, and Eliza considered them a total waste of time. In Charles Town she and her women friends sometimes played whist, but the wagers, if any, were minimal.

In June 1753, fellow South Carolinian Peter Manigault wrote his mother from his English school about Colonel Pinckney, with whom he had visited: "He already seems to have some desire to return to Carolina and I daresay he will, sooner than he at first talked of.... His wife is an excellent woman and I venture to say would choose to pass her days in England; however, she is too good a wife ever to thwart her husband's inclination."

Colonel Pinckney apparently shared Eliza's view about the large sums wagered at England's card tables, as young Manigault continued, "He seems a little better reconciled to England, but can't bring himself to play Whist for crowns."

When war resumed between England and France, the Pinckneys set sail for South Carolina. After a ten-week ocean voyage, they reached Charleston in May 1758.

Within a few weeks of their return, Colonel Pinckney died, on July 12, 1758, after contracting malaria. He and Eliza were visiting the Jacob Mottes at Mount Pleasant, where they had gone to escape the intense heat on the South Carolina mainland. His funeral was held in their home church of Saint Philip's in Charleston, and he was buried in the church cemetery. A large crowd attended.

Eliza was deeply grieved by his death, but she had to keep busy with her husband's several plantations, as well as keep watch over her father's property.

She was now responsible entirely for rearing three young children and seeing that they received an education. The plantations had suffered during their absence, and she had to spend much time trying to restore them. She wrote her father, "I find it requires great care and attention to attend to a Carolina estate, though but a moderate one and to do one's duty, and make all turn to account."

Eliza realized she would have to enlist help in running the plantations and she hired a competent planter to direct the activities of the overseers. The properties were scattered and a recent long-term drought had brought on several financial problems. In a letter to their London business agent, she wrote, "All that we make from ye planting interest will hardly defray ye charges of ye plantations."

Eliza worked diligently, and soon the Pinckney economic affairs were in better condition. When her sons were old enough to enter school in England, she sent them there to be educated.

She wrote faithfully to her sons and missed them, but her letters were not heavy with sentiment. The boys were given advice about proper behavior and assured that she trusted them to do the right thing and that they could learn any subject if they worked hard and tried.

As they matured, Eliza continued to be supportive, but she did not interfere in matters that required them to exercise their own best judgment. Both sons graduated from Oxford University and became lawyers.

All their education took years, and Eliza did not see her son Charles Cotesworth again until he was 23 years old; she did not see Thomas until he was 22 years old. All their teen years had been spent in England. Even so, both Charles and Thomas responded to the call for soldiers during the Revolution. Thomas served in the Army, and Charles served as an aide to General George Washington.

Both sons fought against the British invasion of Charleston, and Thomas received a serious wound in his leg. Harriott's husband, Daniel Horry, had also joined forces resisting the British invaders. (Harriott was educated in Charles Town and at age 19 Harriott had married Daniel Horry, owner of a rice plantation in South Carolina named Hampton Place.)

Thomas's leg would not heal, and at last he and his wife, Betsy Motte, were allowed to take their baby son, Tom, into Charleston to stay in the Horrys' townhouse on Broad Street.

Charles Cotesworth Pinckney and his wife, the former Sally Middleton, lost two baby sons to malaria in 1779 and 1780. Eliza's home had been damaged during the British occupation of it, with everything inside destroyed. Moreover, cattle had been killed to feed British soldiers, and large old oak trees had been cut for use as firewood. When Harriott and Daniel Horry went back to Hampton (their plantation on the Santee River), Eliza went with them.

Charles aided in the establishment of the new United States government as a member of the Continental Congress in 1787, at which he represented South Carolina.

Thomas inherited his grandfather's and mother's interest in agriculture. He sought to improve the quality of the cattle he owned by cross-breeding them with imported cattle of other breeds from England and Italy. He also had dikes built on Pinckney property to hold back seawater so rice could be cultivated in their farm fields.

Thomas served as governor of South Carolina from 1787 to 1789.

At first Eliza was torn by conflicting loyalties during the Revolutionary War because she had many friends and relatives in England. Both of her sons, however, were adamant in their belief that the colonies should have their independence from British rule, and Eliza adopted their point of view in time.

British authorities had confiscated Eliza's home at Charles Town during their occupation of that city, and she despaired of ever returning to a normal life, but she did finally.

Despite Eliza's interests outside her own household through the years, she took great pride in Harriott's homemaking efforts and recognized her other talents.

Not long after Harriott's marriage, Eliza wrote Daniel Horry, "I am glad your little wife looks well to the ways of her household.... The management of a dairy is an amusement she has always been fond of.... I know she has people out gathering simples, different kinds of snake root and pink root and is distilling herbs and flowers."

Eliza lived a quiet life alone in the Pinckney family home after her children married, She continued to experiment with plants, but on a small scale. She was almost bankrupt and had no money with which to restore her property from the war damages it had suffered.

When she was 70 years old, Eliza developed breast cancer, and she went to live with Harriott, whose husband had died recently. Harriott was now successfully managing the Horry family's rice plantation, which was showing a good profit.

On May 1, 1791, President George Washington came to visit Harriott Pinckney Horry and Eliza in Harriott's home. They had been told the day before of his planned visit, and Harriott and Eliza welcomed him warmly.

President Washington was favorably impressed by the Horry rice plantation, and he and Thomas Pinckney reminisced about their adventures during the Revolutionary War.

Harriott had an elegant meal prepared, and the president complimented her on the delicious food. He spent the night in Harriott's home, and went on the next day to Snee Farm of Charles Cotesworth Pinckney, where he was fed an elaborate breakfast.

Eliza went to Philadelphia in April 1793, to visit a cancer doctor. She died there on May 26, 1793. A granddaughter who had gone with her was the only member of her family present when Eliza died.

When Eliza's funeral was held on May 27, 1793, in Philadelphia in Saint Peter's Episcopal Church, President Washington served as a pallbearer, at his own request.

She was buried in Philadelphia.

Eliza Lucas Pinckney proved women are capable and diligent workers, even in jobs previously considered suitable only for men. Her father was wise to give her the opportunity to prove her abilities.

Bibliography

Spruill, Julia Cherry. *Women's Life and Work in the Southern Colonies.* Chapel Hill: University of North Carolina Press, 1938.

Williams, Frances Leigh. *A Founding Family: The Pinckneys of South Carolina.* New York: Harcourt, 1978.

Williams, Selma R. *Dementers Daughters.* New York: Atheneum, 1976.

17

Elizabeth Murray Smith

Elizabeth Murray was owner and operator of her own fashion shop in Boston at a time when the independence of women was not only discouraged, but actually frowned on.

Elizabeth was born in Scotland in 1726 and spent her early years there. When her older brother, James Murray, came to the colony of North Carolina in 1739 to seek his fortune as a planter, Elizabeth came with him to work as his housekeeper, as he was not married. They settled near the Cape River, where they lived for four years.

In 1744 business affairs concerning inheritance required that they return to their old home for a short while. They spent the next five years in Scotland, during which time James married and a daughter was born to him and his wife.

James decided to return to North Carolina in 1749, having settled his affairs in Scotland, and he asked Elizabeth to go back with them.

Before she left, Elizabeth bought a supply of cloth, thread, buttons, lace, needles and other sewing accessories, planning to set up a small business of her own when she reached North Carolina and the home that she and James had occupied previously. James financed the purchases for her shop.

Elizabeth had second thoughts about going back to live with James and his new family in North Carolina, and when their ship docked at Boston before sailing south to the North Carolina colony,

Elizabeth disembarked, explaining that she had decided to open a shop in Boston.

By 1751 Elizabeth was ready for business. She posted a notice mentioning that she was the proprietor of a shop that sold varieties of cloth, sewing notions, women's jewelry, gloves, hose and women's shoes. The notice also announced she would rent rooms, board young women and teach sewing.

Three years later Elizabeth was showing a profit in her enterprises, despite writing her brother that people laughed at her business knowledge and methods of bookkeeping. She told him she had hired a woman to assist her in the shop and that she had decided to go to England to learn proper business procedures.

Elizabeth had an inventory valued at £700 in her Boston shop, but while she was in England she decided millinery would be a worthwhile addition to her other endeavors, and she bought millinery supplies so she could make hats for style-conscious ladies in Boston, showing them the latest fashions in vogue in London.

Not long after her return to Boston in 1755, Elizabeth married Thomas Campbell, an emigrant from Scotland now engaged in working as a Boston merchant also.

Elizabeth requested James' permission to marry, even though she was 29 years old. James wrote their brother John, still in Scotland, that he had granted Elizabeth's request, "not doubting of her having accepted the best that offered and considering she had not much time to wait for further choice."

Massachusetts law at that time stated that married women could not make contracts as individuals or own property without the consent of their husbands, unless they had executed a written agreement between them before marriage. No record has been found of such an agreement between Elizabeth and her new husband, and apparently she closed her business for a time after her marriage.

James Murray sent his young daughter, Dolly, now 10 years old, to Boston to live with Elizabeth and her new husband the same year they married. James wanted Elizabeth to supervise Dolly's education in Boston.

In 1758 James' wife died, and soon after he brought a younger daughter, Betsy, and a niece named Anne Clark to live with Elizabeth and her husband in Boston. Anne Clark was Elizabeth's sister's child. Elizabeth found herself a surrogate mother to three young girls.

She devoted much time and interest to the activities of the children. With Dolly she focused on teaching her writing and accounting skills she had learned in England, telling Dolly, "We will see if your Papa will let you keep his books. The learning of it as they do at school is nothing without the practice. How many families are ruined by women not understanding accounts!"

Anne Clark proved to be an excellent reader and was an avid student of geography. Betsy Murray became too proud of academic abilities, and according to one of Elizabeth's friends, Betsy was "always Sensible Above her years, but at one time she was told too much of it" and "was affected by the most dangerous sort of vanity."

The next year, in 1759, Thomas Campbell died, and a short time later Elizabeith reentered the business world. As a widow she had no restrictions and could operate a business freely as a single woman.

When Elizabeth married for a second time in 1760, she and her new husband, named James Smith, signed a prenuptial agreement which gave her full control over her own property. The agreement also granted Elizabeth the right to make a will of her own, which was not a right given to all wives. Under the agreement, Elizabeth would receive a cash settlement at her husband's death, but she relinquished all other dower rights.

James Smith was a wealthy 70-year-old Boston distiller. Elizabeth did not need to work for financial gain, but she missed her shop and the contact with her customers. She wrote her friend Christine Barnes in Marlborough, "I prefer a useful member of society to all the fine delicate creatures of the age."

During the next few years Elizabeth became aware of how taxation policies of the British government were beginning to irritate her Boston friends and neighbors. The Stamp Act passed by the British parliament was burdensome, requiring any newspaper, legal document or other business paper in any colony to have a document stamp affixed. The prices of the stamps ranged from a half-penny to as much as 20 shillings.

Virginia colonists, led by Patrick Henry, protested vehemently about the new law, and riots occurred in Boston as time passed. Strangely the heavy-handed tax laws of the British government united the colonists in a way nothing else could have done: Now all the colonies had a common enemy whose name was England.

Parliament hastily reconsidered its actions, and the Stamp Act was rescinded. But the colonists realized that English officials were demonstrating their power to impose taxes on the colonists in any way and at any time they chose. Elizabeth was dismayed by the lack of judgment shown by members of Parliament, but she took no active part in the discussions.

Elizabeth hired a young woman named Janette Day as an assistant in her Boston shop. Janette was from Britain, and she had come to America after she gave birth to an illegitimate daughter she named Jackie. Elizabeth had sympathy for the young woman and wanted to help her. She soon discovered Janette was too capable in business to remain a clerk for long. She asked Janette if she would like to teach sewing. Janette was thrilled that someone wanted to help her, and Elizabeth loaned her money to open her own small sewing school. The school was a success from the start, and Janette gradually regained "that Internal Satisfaction I had lost by my own folly."

When a close friend of Elizabeth's died and left her two daughters, Anne and Betsy Cuming, complete orphans, Elizabeth financed their venture in a fancy needlework shop, which attracted patrons from the wealthy women in Boston. The Cuming girls, like Janette, were successful in their enterprise. Anne Cuming wrote Elizabeth in

1769, "You directed us in the way that would most contribute to our mutual happiness, without considering how much your interest might suffer in trusting your property in the hands of two young inexperienced girls ... You kindly contrived to keep us together and made us independent of everyone but yourself.... What should we have been without such a friend?"

Elizabeth's second husband died in 1769, and she was deeply grieved. She was forced to suspend operation of her shop and devote her time and energy to the settlement of Mr. Smith's current business affairs and her own. She received a cash settlement of £10,000 from his estate, as their agreement had specified.

Elizabeth became severely depressed after her husband's death. Later that year, Betsy Murray, who continued in her willful stubborn ways, was sent by Elizabeth to Edinburgh, Scotland, and was entered in a boarding school there to learn discipline. The change of scene helped Elizabeth regain some of her old optimism.

Anne Clark had married in 1769, and she moved with her new husband to North Carolina. James Murray did not like William Hooper, Anne's husband, at all, but Anne ignored her uncle's objections, and the marriage proved to be a success. Hooper studied law and eventually became one of the signers of the Declaration of Independence.

Also in 1769, Dolly Murray married clergyman John Forbes, and the couple went to live in St. Augustine, located in the East Florida territory, which was under British control.

After getting Betsy settled in her new school, Elizabeth went to visit her brother John and his family who lived in England, staying with them until 1771.

While staying in John's home, Elizabeth became interested in John's oldest child, a daughter named Mary but called Polly. Polly had been a student in a boarding school for the past six years, and Elizabeth told John she thought Polly should enter the business world and not "enter the gay scenes of life and become a fine lady." Elizabeth wanted Polly to go with her back to Boston and work as a clerk in the shop of the Cuming sisters.

British Parliament members were slow in learning the folly of imposing onerous levies on the American colonists. When the Townshend Acts were enacted in 1772, citizens in Boston and elsewhere felt they had been pushed beyond their limits of tolerance.

On December 16, 1773, about 150 men and boys, who were minimally disguised as Indians, dumped 342 chests of taxed tea into the Boston harbor. The amount represented the total cargo of three ships. From that time on, colonial resistance to British rule and taxation grew. There would be no compromise this time.

As with all disputes between government officials and ordinary citizens, the effects were felt by everyone. In Boston patriots began a surveillance of merchants to prevent the importation of British-made goods into Massachusetts for resale. In November 1769, the Cumings girls had a visit from the patriot committee, who insisted the girls had violated the pact against imports when they received a shipment of merchandise for their shop three days before. Betsy Cuming wrote Elizabeth, still in England, "we have never entered into any agreement...." She said she felt the authorities should not "try to injur two industrious girls who were striving in an honest way to get their bread."

Despite the burgeoning difficulties, Polly Murray left England in early 1770 with merchandise valued at £300 and plans to open her own hat shop. Polly would first work for the Cumings girls to learn accounting methods so she could keep her own accounts later.

James Murray moved to Boston to assist his niece with opening her new business, but more than a year passed before political conditions were settled enough to allow it.

Elizabeth married for a third time in 1771, not long after her return to Massachusetts. Her new husband, Ralph Inman, was a retired merchant who had begged Elizabeth to marry him before she went to England.

Elizabeth discovered that because of the unrest in Massachusetts and the lack of trade with England, the value of her inheritance from James Smith had diminished in value while she was overseas. She believed her new husband could advise her about business affairs.

The prenuptial agreement between Elizabeth and Inman was more explicit in guaranteeing Elizabeth's control over her own property than the one she and Mr. Smith had signed ten years earlier. Under the new agreement, her husband would receive the interest, income and profits from Elizabeth's property, but nothing else. The newlyweds went to live on Mr. Inman's farm in Cambridge, Massachusetts.

With Elizabeth as their financial backer, Polly and Ann Murray, along with young Jackie Day, opened a hat-making shop in Boston in 1772. Ann and Jackie fashioned the hats, while Polly served the customers and kept the accounts in order. The arrangement did not work. Ann and Polly became homesick for their parents and England, and Jackie found it was impossible for her to carry on the business alone. She later married.

When the Revolutionary War started in 1775, Dolly and Betsy were staying at Cambridge with Elizabeth. Dolly had recently arrived from Florida for a visit with her aunt and sister. Ralph Inman was in Boston on a business matter and could not get back home.

General George Washington took command of Continental armed forces on July 3, 1775, in Cambridge, and most women and children fled from the area. Elizabeth and her nieces decided to remain on the Inman farm. Elizabeth had been caring for the farm in her husband's absence and there was a good crop of hay standing in the fields. The women meant to get the hay crop harvested, as they knew the Continental soldiers would need the hay to feed their horses.

Elizabeth wrote Ralph about their circumstances: "I throw my anxiety off with a laugh, go about and order things as if I was to stay here for years.... As we have sown it is a pity not to reap."

Ralph was not brave like his wife. In fact, by the end of July that year he was in a panic in Boston. He wrote Elizabeth that he wanted to sail to England as soon as he could secure passage. He wanted no part of a war and he accused his wife of being a rebel sympathizer and supporter. When she received his letter, Elizabeth was shocked. She could not believe he would accuse her of aiding and abetting rebels. He knew her feelings about a revolution were ambivalent since her brother James had recently been forced to leave Boston because of his loyalist views.

Elizabeth wrote Ralph, "Be assured, Dear Sir, I will with pleasure account for every action that I remember since ... the year of my birth.... Believe me, Mr. Inman, I am not anxious about maintenance. Experience has taught me water-gruel and salt for supper and breakfast with a bit of meat and a few greens or roots are enough for me."

Perhaps Elizabeth's scorn was enough to cause Ralph to rethink matters; he did not go to England after all. He came back to his Cambridge farm in 1776, but Elizabeth never forgave him for his willingness to desert her during wartime.

By 1783 Elizabeth had decided the colonists had been right in their decision to overthrow British rule and form their own government. She wrote her brother John that she was surprised by the business success she had enjoyed in Massachusetts and that "my heart overflows with gratitude."

The Cuming sisters moved to Nova Scotia in 1783, having grown tired of living under close scrutiny by patriots at all times and meeting such difficulty obtaining supplies for their shop.

When Elizabeth became terminally ill in May 1785, she made a will in which she left Ralph Inman only £100 a year income for life. He would receive this only after he gave her executors "all the goods, chattels and Estate of which at my decease he shall be possessed in my right."

She had good reasons for her punitive actions against Ralph.

Betsy Murray wrote her cousin Polly early in 1785 that Ralph was greedy and gave Elizabeth "more trouble than her friends are aware of, and his failings are daily increasing...."

Elizabeth made large bequests to her nieces and good friends, with Polly and Ann Murray her residuary legatees.

Ralph was incensed by Elizabeth's dispersal of her property. Betsy wrote Polly that "he alternately curses your family and ours ... because he has not got the whole of the estate or such part of it as he requested." Ralph also made his displeasure felt by refusing to turn over Elizabeth's property to her executor for almost a year, proving that Elizabeth did understand what he might do after her death. Finally, in February 1786, he complied, and his annuity payments began.

Elizabeth's real legacy was beyond Ralph's reach. It was the beneficial influence and encouragement she provided to her nieces and other young women she encountered during her life. She taught them to consider themselves persons in their own right, and she pushed them toward education and training, which would insure their own independence allowing them to marry, should they choose to do so, for love instead of financial support.

Bibliography

Benson, Mary Sumner. *Women in Eighteenth Century America*. New York: Columbia University Press, 1935

Berkin, Carol Ruth, and Mary Beth Norton. *Women of America: A History*. Boston, Mass.: Houghton Mifflin, 1979.

Williams, Selma R. *Dementers Daughters*. New York: Atheneum, 1976.

18

Ann Lee

When Ann Lee arrived in America on board the *Mariah* from Manchester, England, in May 1774, she came as one of the founders of a religious sect begun in 1758 by dissenting Quakers. The new group was known as the Shakers because of their exuberant form of worship — they trembled and shook, danced and shouted.

Ann was born Ann *Lees*—later dropping the *s*—on February 29, 1736, in Manchester, to John Lees and his wife, whose name is not known. Ann was one of eight children, having five brothers and two sisters. John Lees was a blacksmith and barely made enough to feed his family, so Ann never had an opportunity to attend school.

When she was about 14, Ann went to work 14 hours a day in a textile mill where she was a good worker. Later she worked as a cook at an infirmary in Manchester.

From early childhood Ann insisted she had visions of "heavenly things," and she gave much thought to learning God's will for her life.

In 1758 she joined with Jane and James Wardley, local tailors, former Quakers who were now engaged in trying to convince their fellow citizens that Christ would soon return to earth and that man should turn away from his sins. Ann remained a member of the Church of England during this time.

In 1762 Ann's relatives urged her to marry Abraham Stanley, a blacksmith employed by her father. They were married in the Anglican Church on January 5, 1752, and went to live with her father and some of her brothers and sisters still living at home. Ann's mother had died several years before.

Ann and Abraham had four children born to them during the next few years — three died in infancy, and a fourth, a daughter, died at age six. Ann's own health also suffered as a result of rapid childbearing.

Ann was distraught about the deaths of her children, and she became convinced she was being punished for what she perceived as a sin in having a sexual relationship with her husband. She decided all such activity caused all the evils in the world, and she began preaching total chastity.

Millennialism had taken hold first in France, among the Cevenold Protestants. When the Edict of Nantes, which guaranteed religious freedom, was revoked in October 1685, these dissenting Christians fled to England, where the Wardleys had been predicting the end of time and the downfall of the Antichrist since 1747. The dissenters from France and the Wardleys found their beliefs were alike, and they joined together in a prophesying evangelical group.

Jane Wardley explained to Ann, who had been desperately seeking answers in her own life, that Jane and her husband, James, could only be good friends. They lived together in the same house but did not touch each other.

Ann welcomed Jane's advice and told her own husband, Abraham, that she would no longer share a marriage bed with him. Abraham was not happy about Ann's decision, but he joined in worship with her in the new Shaker society.

Ann had found a cause in which she believed, and she was zealous in its promotion. According to contemporaries, Ann was an attractive woman, but not beautiful, being short in stature and somewhat stocky in build. She had chestnut brown hair, a fair complexion and striking blue eyes. Apparently, she had charisma as well, for she soon assumed leadership in the Shaker Movement, and became known as "Mother Ann" because of the "heavenly" visions she claimed to experience. Believing women and men to be equal in God's sight she placed women in leadership roles, making Ann a pioneer feminist.

Ann and three of her followers were arrested in Manchester in 1772 and again in July 1773, and charged with disturbing the peace. They had gone into the Christ Church in Manchester on Sunday morning and attempted to tell the worshippers of their errors in their beliefs. Onlookers, however, considered the group's passionate dancing and shaking to be blasphemy.

Ann was put in prison for her efforts and later incorporated the story of her captivity in her testimony:

> They put me into the stone prison, and there kept me fourteen days, where I could not straighten myself. The door was never opened through the whole time. ... I had nothing to eat or drink. ...
>
> After I had been there awhile, one of the Believers came and whispered to me, through the key-hole (for he durst not speak a loud word, for fear of being heard), and (he) said, "Put your mouth to the key-hole, and I will give you drink."
>
> I did so, but the pipe-stem was so big he could not get it through the key-hole — so I got no drink that night.
>
> The next night he came again, and put the stem of a pipe through, so that I could just take it into my lips; and I sucked through the pipe-stem till I felt refreshed. It was wine and milk, poured through the bowl of the pipe.
>
> This I received as a favor of God. I had no one to look to, but God, for help. ...
>
> I suffered great persecution in England, on account of my faith.

On a Saturday night as Ann was traveling to a meeting, she and the people with her sat down along the roadside to eat the food they had brought with them. While there Ann had a vision of America in which a tree was covered with brightly shining leaves, which she believed represented the Church of Christ, which she could establish in America.

John Hocknell, one of Ann's followers, was a wealthy man, and he promised to pay the fares to America on the ship *Mariah* for anyone who wished to go and work with Ann. The group left England on May 19, 1774. Eight People traveled with Ann: Her husband Abraham Stanley, who had stayed with Ann during the years; John Hocknell and his son Richard; Ann's brother William and niece Nancy Lee; a young weaver named James Whittaker, who had given Ann the drink while she was in prison earlier; and James Shepherd and Mary Partington.

It was a turbulent trip. First, their manner of worship, with singing, shouting, dancing and shaking, led the captain of the ship to threaten to throw all of them overboard. Second, a violent storm arose, knocking a plank loose on the ship and causing it to take on water. The crew worked frantically pumping out water for a time, but Ann told the captain not to fear. She had seen "two bright angels standing at the mast," and she was sure they would reach New York safely.

Suddenly, a huge wave slapped the plank back into position, and the water stopped pouring in. The *Mariah* reached New York on August 6, 1774.

After their landing, the Shakers walked together up Pearl Street until they reached the home of a Mrs. Cunningham. Ann got a job working for her and her neighbors as a washerwoman, and Ann's husband found work as a blacksmith. John Hocknell went north to a tract of land he had leased from a Dutchman, and later he brought his wife from England to join him.

Abraham's health suffered from the hard work he had to do as a smithy, and Ann was forced to quit her job and take care of him.

They suffered severely from a lack of money while he was ill, until Mr. and Mrs. Hocknell insisted that Ann go with them up the Hudson River to Niskayuna, a community of Shakers eight miles from Albany.

Abraham Stanley had renounced the Shakers after he recovered from his ailment, and he moved in with a woman reported to be a prostitute.

It was 1776, and the Shakers, having come from England, were viewed with suspicion by their neighbors, but they were unaware of any hostility. They continued to clear land, drain the swamp and build log houses. They also continued to gather for their religious meetings, at which they sang, danced, shook and prayed.

For the next four years the Shakers continued undeterred, to live and worship, but few new members were added to their number.

As the Revolutionary War dragged on, however, citizens sought divine aid and guidance for their woes. Hearing of the Shakers, who promised an end to the war, freedom from sin and the imminent return of Christ to earth, the people flocked to the Shaker meetings, and new members were added.

Ann preached to the people that they should give their hearts to God and put their hands to work. She insisted there would be "no dirt in Heaven," and she and her followers kept heir homes orderly and well-scrubbed, and their shops and farms were models of superb upkeep.

Ann told her disciples to "dress yourself in modest apparel ... and teach your family to do likewise." The Shakers dressed in drab-colored plain clothing similar in style to Quaker attire.

Before the influx of new members, Ann and her eldresses, as her women helpers were called, had difficulty keeping their common house clean enough and struggled to cook enough food for strangers who came by for instruction, to visit or for solace. With more hands to work, the Shakers began taking in orphaned and unwanted children, with their own emphasis on celibacy, members would otherwise have no children to later assume the duties of the present members.

In 1780 local authorities detained Ann for several months believing her a British sympathizer because of her pacifist views. But there was no evidence to convict her, and she was released.

New Shaker communities eventually appeared in all of the New England states, as well as Kentucky, Ohio, New York, Florida and Georgia.

In May 1781, Ann and five of the elders embarked on a missionary trip to take their message to both converts and non-believers throughout New England. They visited 36 towns and villages in the New England states and New York area before they finished.

They used a Square House they bought for $568.48 in Harvard, Massachusetts, for their headquarters and visited nearby villages for meetings. They traveled around for two years and were subjected to insults and abuse from people whose relatives had joined the Shakers, from some who believed Mother Ann was a witch and from some who considered the Shaker form of worship to be "heathenish."

The Shakers were noted for their fine craftsmanship of plain furniture of functional design. They were inventors of the ordinary clothespin, a tongue-and-groove machine for dressing lumber, a threshing machine for grain crops, an improved washing machine, and legend has it that an eldress made the first circular saw.

The hard work they did daily and the abuse Ann and the elders suffered took its toll on their health. They went back to Niskayuna in 1783, and a few months later, Ann's beloved brother William died at age 44 from a skull fracture he had received from a beating by an irate citizen.

Ann prophesied: "The time will come when the church will be gathered into order; but not until after my decease," indicating she had a premonition she did not have much time left to live.

As she was dying, Ann told her caretakers she saw her brother William in a vision. He was coming for her in a "glorious chariot." She died at Niskayuna on September 7, 1784, at age 48, and was buried two days later in the Shaker cemetery there. She left her good friend James Whittaker in charge of her group of followers.

There are places today where Shakers and their way of life can still be found. There is a museum at Hancock, Massachusetts, where old buildings, gardens and shops are on display. Two restored villages in Pleasant Hill and South Union, Kentucky, can also be visited by tourists.

In Canterbury, New Hampshire, and Sabbathy Lake, Maine, thriving villages are still peopled by Shakers.

Bibliography

Desroche, Henri. *The American Shakers.* Translated by John Savacool. Amherst, Mass.: University of Massachusetts, 1971

Morse, Flo. *The Shakers and the World's People.* New York: Dodd, Mead and Company, 1980

_____. *The Story of the Shakers.* Woodstock, Vt.: Countryman, 1986.

Neidle, Cecyle S. *America's Immigrant Women.* New York: Hippocrene, 1975.

19

Anne Dudley Bradstreet

Anne Dudley Bradstreet has the distinction of being the first female poet in the American colonies. Her poems were a reflection of her daily life and experiences and were composed for her own pleasure and that of her family. A volume of her poetry was published in 1650 in London when Anne's brother-in-law had submitted them for publication without the knowledge or consent of Anne.

Anne Dudley was born in 1612 in Northampton, England, probably to Thomas and Dorothy Yorke Dudley. When she was seven years old, she and her family went to live on the large estates of the earl of Lincoln in Sempringham, Lincolnshire, where Anne's father was employed as the steward in charge of the estates.

Living in luxurious Tattershall Castle, Anne was taught by private tutors and was allowed access to the earl's private library. It was there she was exposed to great literature of the world including the poetry of Guillaume du Bartas of France and Puritan poet John Milton.

In 1628 when Anne was 16 years old, she married Simon Bradstreet, also a steward on the earl's estate. He was nine years older than his new bride, and the son of a nonconformist minister in England. Simon had been educated at Emmanuel College at Cambridge, from which he graduated.

In 1630, Anne, Simon, and Anne's parents boarded the ship

Arbella, flagship of John Winthrop's fleet to come to the New World to make their home. John Winthrop would be the governor of the new colony they would establish, and Anne's father, Thomas Dudley, would be the deputy governor of the Massachusetts Bay Colony.

Anne came willingly with her husband and parents, but she was shocked by the differences in her old home and her new surroundings. She said, "My heart rose, but after I was convinced it was the way of God, I submitted to it and joined the Church at Boston." Anne realized she had led a sheltered life at the earl's castle where green fields were plentiful, shops were nearby and life's necessities could be purchased. In her new location there were only a few houses and few, if any, of life's more pleasant trappings. It is no wonder that her "heart rose" when she viewed her primitive surroundings.

Anne and Simon camped at Charlestowne while their house at Newtowne was being built. Anne became ill, probably from exposure, leaving her with "a lameness" for a time. Her health had always been delicate, and she was not ideally suited physically to be a pioneer.

Deputy Governor Dudley also built his family's home at Newtowne, and John Winthrop criticized the Dudley house as being too elaborate, but Anne must have enjoyed having her family nearby where she could pay frequent visits.

One of Anne's causes of unhappiness in her new home was that she and Simon had not been able to start their family. When the other women in the colony met at religious services or at other gatherings, the subject of pregnancies and children arose as a natural topic of conversation. Anne, in fact, did not become pregnant for three years, but at last, in 1633, she presented Simon with their first son, whom they named Samuel.

Anne wrote, "It pleased God to keep me a long time without a child, which was a great grief to me." She made up for lost time, however, as Anne eventually gave birth to a total of eight children.

Shortly after Samuel's birth, the Bradstreets moved to a new colony called Ipswich, founded by John Winthrop, Jr. It was then that Anne began writing poetry. Concerning her children, she wrote

> I had eight birds hatcht in one nest;
> Four cocks there were, and Hens the rest,
> I nursed them up with pain and care,
> Nor cost nor labor did I spare,
> Till at last they felt their wing,
> Mounted the trees, and learn'd to sing....

Puritan believers frowned on drama and most other art forms as decadent, but fortunately for Anne, poetry was not forbidden. She was allowed and even encouraged to continue writing her verses, unhindered by her understanding husband and her doting father. Deputy Governor Dudley was not hesitant about expressing his disapproval of some of the activities of his fellow colonists, but he saw no faults in his beloved daughter.

Possibly some Bradstreet neighbors or relatives believed Anne should spend more time executing her household duties or mothering her children and less time writing poetry. The following verse may have been written in defense of her actions:

> I am obnoxious to each carping tongue,
> Who say my hand a needle better fits.
> A Poet's pen all scorn I should thus wrong,
> For such despite they cast on Female wits;
> If what I do prove well, it won't advance,
> They'll say it's stolen, or else it was by chance.

When the controversy about religion swirled around Anne Hutchinson later on, Anne Bradstreet questioned the actions of the Puritan movement and wondered how the men who started it could be so sure they were right. It may have been during this period of her life that she wrote the poem she called "The Flesh and the Spirit," which concerns the eternal struggle between Godliness and human temptation:

In secret place where once I stood
Close by the banks of Lacrim flood,
I heard two sisters reason on
Things that are past and things to come.
One Flesh was called, who had her eye
On worldly wealth and vanity;
The other Spirit, who did rear
Her thoughts unto a higher sphere.
Sister, quoth Flesh, what liv'st thou on —
Nothing but meditation?
Doth contemplation feed thee, so
Regardlessly to let earth go?
Can speculation satisfy
Notion without reality?
Dost dream of things beyond the moon,
And dost thou hope to dwell there soon?
Hast treasures there laid up in store,
That all in th' world thou count'st but poor?
Art fancy sick, or turned a sot,
To catch at shadows which are not?
Come, come, I'll show unto thy sense
Industry hath its recompense.
What canst desire but thou mayst see
True substance in variety?
Dost honor like? Acquire the same,
As some to their immortal fame,
And trophies to thy name erect
Which wearing time shall ne'er deject.
For riches dost thou long full sore?
Behold enough of precious store;
Earth hath more silver, pearls and gold
Than eyes can see or hands can hold.
Affect'st thou pleasure? Take thy fill;
Earth hath enough of what you will.
Then let not go what thou mayest find
For thing unknown, only in mind.

Spirit answered:

Be still, thou unregenerate part:
Disturb no more my settled heart,

For I have vowed (and so will do)
Thee as a foe still to pursue,
And combat with thee will and must
Until I see Thee laid in th' dust.
. . . .
I'll stop mine ears at these thy charms
And count them for my deadly harms.
Thy sinful pleasures I do hate,
Thy riches are to me no bait,
Thine honors do nor will I love,
For my ambition lies above.
. . . .
Nor are they shadows which I catch,
Nor fancies vain at which I snatch:
. . . .
Mine eye doth pierce the heavens, and see
What is invisible to thee.
My garments are not silk nor gold
Nor such like trash which earth doth hold,
But royal robes I shall have on
More glorious than the glist'ring sun.
My crown not diamonds, pearls, and gold,
But such as angels heads enfold.
The city where I hope to dwell
There's none on earth can parallel;
. . . .
The streets thereof transparent gold,
Such as no eye did e'er behold;
A crystal river there doth run,
Which doth proceed from the Lamb's throne;
. . . .
Nor withering age shall e'er come there,
But beauty shall be bright and clear.
This city pure is not for thee,
For things unclean there shall not be.
If I of heaven may have my fill,
Take thou the world, and all that will.

About 1650 the Bradstreets moved again to a new home in a new village, now known as Andover, where they lived and thrived in contentment. After living for 16 years in a house that she had considered her real home, Anne watched a fire burn it to the ground in 1666.

As was her habit, Anne expressed her deepest feelings in verse. In "Upon the Burning of Our House, July 10, 1666," she wrote,

When by the ruins oft I passed
My sorrowing eyes aside did cast,
And here and there the places spy
Where oft I sat, and long did lie.
. . . .
My pleasant things in ashes lie,
And them behold no more shall I.
Under thy roof no guest shall sit,
Nor at thy table eat a bit.
. . . .
In silence ever shalt thou lie:
Adieu, adieu, all's vanity.

Despite evidence that Anne Bradstreet was subjected to ill-natured gossip, all her children matured into worthwhile citizens. Samuel, the oldest son, studied medicine in England and became a doctor in Jamaica. Her daughter, Dorothy, married the son of the Reverend John Cotton and was himself a minister. Sarah married her brother's classmate Richard Hubbard. Dudley Bradstreet became a soldier, and Simon, Jr., became a minister in New London, Connecticut. The remaining three, Hanna, John and Mercy, were all respected and active church members.

Anne's brother-in-law the Reverend John Woodbridge took some of Anne's poetry to London, where it was published in 1650 under the title *The Tenth Muse Lately Sprung Up in America, or Several Poems, Compiled with Great Variety of Wit and Learning, Full of Delight ... By a Gentlewoman of Those Parts.*

Anne was pleased by the attention her poetry received, but while she continued writing poems, she made no effort to compile a second volume. As she aged, Anne's health deteriorated, and she died on September 16, 1672, possibly of tuberculosis.

Anne and Simon Bradstreet had been married for 44 years, and their union had been happy. She wrote a tribute to him entitled "To My Dear and Loving Husband,":

If ever two were one, then surely we.
If ever man were loved by wife, then thee.
If ever wife was happy in a man,
Compare with me, ye women, if you can.
I prize thy love more than whole mines of gold,
Or all the riches that the East doth hold.
My love is such that rivers cannot quench,
Nor ought but love from thee give recompense.
Thy love is such I can no way repay;
The heavens reward thee manifold, I pray.
Then while we live, in love let's so persevere
That when we live no more, we may live ever.

Bibliography

James, Edward T., Janet W. James, and Paul S. Boyer. In *Notable American Women*. "Anne Bradstreet." Vol. 1. Cambridge, Mass.: Harvard University Press, Belknap Press, 1971.

Miller, Perry, ed. *The American Puritans: Their Prose and Poetry*. New York: Columbia University Press, 1956.

Morrison, Samuel Eliot. *Builders of the Bay Colony*. Boston Mass.: Houghton Mifflin, 1962.

20

Jane Randolph Jefferson

Jane Randolph would have had no hint while she was a young girl that she would someday have a son who would help found a nation. That son, Thomas Jefferson, would go down in history as one of the greatest presidents of the United States.

Jane was born in London in Shadwell parish in 1720 to a sea captain and his wife, Isham and Jane Rodgers Randolph. Mrs. Randolph was stern and strict, according to historical accounts, and since little Jane was her firstborn child, all her parental guiding instincts were employed to their fullest.

Captain Randolph had been educated at William and Mary College in the Virginia colony, and eventually he brought his ever-increasing family back to Virginia to make their home. Engaged in the profitable slave-trading of the times, he soon became a wealthy man who provided an imposing mansion for his family's home.

In October 1739, at the age of 19, Jane Randolph married Peter Jefferson in Virginia. Peter was descended from Welsh forebears but belonged to the third generation of Virginia settlers. Peter was 31 and had been busy acquiring a 400-acre tract of land along the Rivanna River for a plantation homestead.

Peter built a home for his bride on their new plantation, and there their first son, whom they named Thomas, was born on April 13, 1743. A daughter, named for her mother, had been born in 1740, and the little girl lost no time in appointing herself the protector of her baby brother.

The plantation was called Shadwell in honor of Jane's old home parish in London. Jane's family was unimpressed by her new home, however, describing it as "a small clearing in dense and primeval forest."

In 1745, Jane Jefferson's brother, William Randolph, asked Jane and Peter if they could move their family to his plantation to help him care for his motherless children, as his wife had died recently. His own health was not good, and he felt unequal to caring for three children alone.

Jane and Peter uprooted their family and moved to William's plantation, called Tuckahoe, where they lived for the next seven years. It was well they had gone, for William Randolph died a few months after they joined him.

At Tuckahoe, Jane cared for her two nieces and nephew, all older than her own children, and continued to give birth to children of her own eventually reaching a total of six daughters and two sons.

She must have had a busy, difficult life, even with slave women to help her. It appears, however she never questioned her duty to help her relatives, especially since Peter Jefferson was the guardian of the Randolph children and had been a close friend of her brother William.

As time passed and the Randolph children grew older, Jane felt they could now care for themselves adequately, and she persuaded Peter they should move back to Shadwell to live.

Peter had continued adding acreage to his own plantation, and he owned about 2,500 acres. He built a new, larger house for his family, as well as needed outbuilding and servants' quarters.

In 1752, Peter Jefferson decided his son Thomas needed more education than he could provide and arranged for the boy, now nine years old, to go to Dover Church, a village located five miles from Tuckahoe and 25 miles from Shadwell. There Thomas could be educated in a classical manner by the Reverend William Douglas.

Jane must have been sad to see her son leave home at such a young age, for he would live with the Douglas family each year during the school term. This arrangement was in place for five years.

In 1757, Thomas returned for the last time from Dover Church. His father had died at age 49, leaving Jane with eight young children to rear alone. They were young Jane, Elizabeth, Lucy, Mary, Martha, twins Anna and Randolph, in addition to Thomas. Peter Jefferson's will gave Jane care and control of Shadwell for her lifetime. As the eldest son, Thomas had to assume the head of the family.

Thomas did not stay home for long, because his education had to be completed. Jane arranged for him to attend a different school in Fredericksville, where he would study with James Maury, an Anglican clergyman. In his new school Thomas could spend weekends at home.

The 14 year-old Thomas spent the next two years with the Maury family, and during this time he developed an antipathy toward the Anglican Church and its power. Whether he disliked his teacher so much as to cause a repudiation of his own family's church or whether it was the common rebellious attitude of a teenager is uncertain.

Jane must have been dismayed by this turn of events, but if she tried to change Thomas's mind, there is no record. She had enough to worry about with her daughter Elizabeth, who was mentally retarded.

As Thomas matured, he had a difficult time deciding what course he should follow in his life. At Shadwell he had friends coming and going frequently, as did his sisters. With so much entertaining, Jane, mindful that she had to be careful with money, complained about the expense.

When Thomas was 19, he decided he would attend the College of William and Mary as his father had many years before. He became interested in the practice of law, and George Wythe was his teacher.

Wythe was a highly respected lawyer in the Virginia colony, and his newest apprentice studied with him for five years. Most students only studied for two years, but Thomas had an insatiable desire for knowledge.

Thomas had assumed the task of keeping financial records for his mother's plantation, and he continued to do so meticulously and accurately.

In 1770 the family mansion at Shadwell was destroyed in a fire. Thomas had started building a house for himself at a place he called Monticello, near Shadwell, but it was not completed. Unfortunately, he had not moved his books and legal papers to his new home, and all were lost in the fire.

Jane and her younger children continued to live at Shadwell after the fire, probably setting up housekeeping in an outbuilding on the plantation.

Jane was described by a granddaughter as witty, vivacious and charming. She was reputed to be an excellent housekeeper, and her present living conditions must have caused her distress. She had many good friends, and some of them may have provided household items.

Two years later, Thomas married Martha Wayles Skelton, and they went to live in the one finished room of his house at Monticello.

It has been speculated that Jane did not approve of her son's choice of wife, and a granddaughter characterized it as "a delicate and difficult situation."

Since Thomas had lived at home until he was 27 and was now 29, Jane may have hoped he would not marry at all. He had been a great help to her in many ways. He was, however, old enough to make his own decisions.

By this time Thomas and a number of his friends and acquaintances began to feel the need for independence from the burdensome rule of Great Britain.

Since Jane Jefferson had been born in England, she had many relatives still living there, and she found the independence movement to be heart-breaking. With Thomas's insistence on breaking away from the English government, she may have felt he was once again rejecting her values.

Also, she may have feared for his physical safety. The treatise he had written entitled "A Summary View of the Rights of British America" could be considered treasonous. He could have been hanged for publishing it.

Jane's daughters were a source of pride and comfort to her as they became adults. Mary married John Bolling, who was a member of the Virginia House of Burgesses. Martha married Dabney Carr, also a member of the House of Burgesses. Lucy married William Lewis. (Their son, Meriwether Lewis, explored the Northwest with George Rogers Clark.)

Jane died unmarried at age twenty-five, probably of smallpox, and Anna married a man named Marks.

On February 21, 1774, the Virginia region suffered a severe earthquake, and it is believed the quake somehow led to the death of Elizabeth Jefferson who was 29 years old. Since she did not have good understanding of events, she may have run away in fear and become lost.

Thomas Jefferson recorded in his account book on March 1, "My sister Elizabeth was found last Thursday, being February 24." On March 7, 1774, he wrote about her funeral, but he provided no explanation of her cause of death.

The increasing clamor in the colonies for independence from England created tension within Jane's family. Her relatives, particularly the Randolphs, as well as some of those in other families, decided to leave Virginia, returning to England to live. John Randolph, Jane's brother, was the attorney general of the Virginia colony, but he also went back to live in England. He sold all his land and other possessions, and removed his family from the treasonous atmosphere. His son Edmund Randolph, however, remained in Virginia, where he served as an aide to General George Washington during the Revolutionary War.

At the age of 33, Edmund became attorney general of the new state of Virginia. Later, he was elected governor of Virginia, was the United State's attorney general during President George Washington's administration and secretary of state during Washington's second term.

All the serious disagreements and unpleasantness among her family members took their toll on Jane Jefferson's health. She died at age 57 on March 31, 1776, after a very brief illness. She was buried at Monticello.

Possibly Thomas Jefferson felt some remorse for the emotional pain he and others had caused his mother, for he developed a severe persistent headache following her death. He was incapacitated for six weeks and was unable to rejoin his colleagues in Philadelphia at the Continental Congress session there.

His mother had always been available to talk to him when he needed her, and she had encouraged him in his development into a responsible citizen and lawyer.

It is sad that Jane did not live to see her son become the third president of the United States.

Bibliography

Brodie, Fawn M. *Thomas Jefferson: An Intimate History.* New York: Bantam, 1974.

Faber, Doris. *The Mothers of American Presidents.* New York: New American Library, 1968.

Peterson, Merrill D. *Thomas Jefferson and The New Nation.* New York: Oxford University Press, 1970.

Randall, Willard Stern. *Thomas Jefferson, a Life.* New York: Henry Holt, 1993.

21

Mary White Rowlandson

Mary White was born in Somersetshire, England, about 1635 to John and Joane West White of South Petherton. Mary was one of their nine children.

The White family left England sometime before 1650 and came to Salem, Massachusetts, to make their home. They went on to live in Lancaster on the frontier in 1653.

Mary found romance in Lancaster, and she married the Reverend Joseph Rowlandson there in 1656. Joseph was the first full-time minister the Lancaster church had. He was a son of Thomas Rowlandson of Ipswich, Connecticut.

Mary and Joseph had a home built on a hill above Ropers Brook, and settled down to married life. Their first child, a daughter named Mary, was born about January 1658, but lived only a short time. Their son Joseph was born March 7, 1661; a second daughter, also named Mary, was born August 12, 1665; and a third daughter named Sarah was born September 15, 1669.

The Wampanoag Indians in the region had been friendly to white settlers from the beginning at Plymouth when Chief Massasoit and his braves showed the newcomers how to plant corn, and how to fish and hunt wild game.

In 1664 Metacom, the son of Massasoit, became the chief of the Wampanoags, and the white settlers began to fear he would stir up trouble for them. He was brought into their courts on several occasions and questioned about the plans of his tribe, but he insisted the white settlers had nothing to fear from his people.

The settlers dubbed Metacom "King Philip" in derision because of his dignified manner. Tensions increased between the settlers and Indians until on June 24, 1675, the Indians raided a white village and 11 white settlers were killed in retaliation for the murder of an Indian man the day before.

For the next several months the Indians engaged in a guerrilla-type war against the settlers, and many villages were attacked and burned. One of the villages was that of the Rowlandson family, and during the raid Mary Rowlandson and her three children were taken captive by the Indians.

Mary wrote of her ordeal many years later in a book entitled *A Narrative of the Captivity and Restoration of Mrs. Mary Rowlandson.* She wrote,

> On the tenth of February, 1676, came the Indians with great numbers upon Lancaster. Their first coming was about sun-rising; hearing the noise of some guns, we looked out; several houses were burning and the smoke ascending to Heaven. There were five persons taken in one house.... There were two others who, being out of their garrison upon some occasion, were set upon; one was knocked on the head, the other escaped. Another ... was ... shot and wounded and fell down.... Another, seeing many of the Indians about his barn, ventured and went out, but was quickly shot down. There were three others belonging to the same garrison who were killed....
>
> At length they came and beset our own house, and quickly it was the dolefulest day that ever mine eyes saw.... About two hours ... they had been about the house before they prevailed to fire it (which they did with flax and hemp which they brought out of the barn...).

The house [was] on fire over our heads, and the bloody heathen ready to knock us on the head if we stirred out.... Then I took my children (and one of my sisters, hers) to go forth and leave the house; but as soon as we came to the door and appeared, the Indians shot so thick that the bullets rattled against the house.

But out we must go, the fire increasing and coming along behind us, roaring.... No sooner were we out of the house but my brother-in-law (being before wounded, in defending the house, in or near the throat) fell down dead.... The bullets flying thick, one went through my side, and the same (as would seem) through the bowels and hand of my dear child in my arms....

Of thirty-seven persons who were in this one house, none escaped either present death or a bitter captivity, save only one.... There were twelve killed; some shot, some stabbed with their spears, some knocked down with their hatchets....

I had often before this said that if the Indians should come I should choose rather to be killed by them than taken alive; but when it came to the trial my mind changed. Their glittering weapons so daunted my spirit that I chose rather to go along with those ... than that moment to end my days....

Now away we must go with those barbarous creatures.... About a mile we went that night, up upon a hill within sight of the town, where they intended to lodge.... This was the dolefulest night that ever my eyes saw.... All was gone; my husband gone (at least separated from me, he being in the Bay — and to add to my grief the Indians told me they would kill him as he came homeward), my children gone, my relations and friends gone, our house and home and all our comforts within doors and without....

There remained nothing to me but one poor wounded babe, and it seemed at present worse than death that it was in such a pitiful condition, bespeaking compassion; and I had no refreshing for it nor suitable things to revive it....

The next morning, I must turn my back upon the town and travel with them into the vast and desolate wilderness, I knew not whither.... One of the Indians carried my poor wounded babe upon a horse; it went moaning all along, "I shall die, I shall die."...

I took it off the horse and carried it in my arms till my strength failed.... Then they set me upon a horse with my wounded child in my lap....

After some hours had passed, "it quickly began to snow, and when night came on, they stopped. And now down I must sit in the snow, by a little fire and [with] a few boughs behind me with my sick child in my lap and calling much for water, being now fallen into a violent fever. My own wound [was] also growing so stiff that I could scarcely sit down or rise up."

Mary referred to their changing camps and locations as "removes." On their third remove,

> The morning being come, they prepared to go on their way.... It may be easily judged what a poor, feeble condition we were in, there being not the least crumb of refreshing that came within either of our mouths from Wednesday night to Saturday night, except only a little cold water....
>
> The next day was the Sabbath.... This day there came to me one Robert Pepper (a man belonging to Roxbury), who was taken in Captain Beers' fight and had been now a considerable time with the Indians and [had gone] up with them most as far as Albany to see King Philip.... He told me he was wounded in the leg ... and he took oaken leaves and laid to his wound and through the blessing of God, he was able to travel again. Then I took oaken leaves and laid to my side, and ... it cured me also.
>
> My child being even ready to depart this sorrowful

> world, they bade me carry it out to another wigwam ...
> whither I went with a very heavy heart.... About two
> hours in the night my sweet babe like a lamb departed
> this life ... it being about six years and five months
> old....

The Indians buried Sarah upon a hill, and they allowed Mary to go
see her grave.

Her captors later allowed the grieving mother to visit, under
close supervision, her other daughter Mary: "I went to see my daughter Mary, who was at this same Indian town at a wigwam not very
far off, though we had little liberty or opportunity to see one another.
She was about ten years old, and taken from the door at first by a
praying Indian and afterward sold for gun."

Mary was not allowed to touch her daughter because she wept
at the sight of her. A short time late, however, her son Joseph was
allowed to visit her.

"My son came to me and asked me how I did," she wrote, "I had
not seen him before, since the destruction to the town, and I knew
not where he was till I was informed by himself that he was amongst
a smaller parcel of Indians, whose place was about six miles off. With
tears in his eyes he asked me whether his sister Sarah was dead, and
told me he had seen his sister Mary, and prayed me that I would not
be troubled in reference to himself...."

The next day the Indians attacked and burned the village of
Medfield.

> One of the Indians that came from the Medfield fight
> had brought some plunder, [and] came to me and asked
> me — if I would have a Bible, he had one in his basket.
> I was glad of it, and asked whether he thought the Indi-
> ans would let me read. He answered, "yes" so I took the
> Bible.... It was my guide by day and my pillow by night.
> Now the Indians began to talk of removing from this
> place, some [going] one way and some another.... Now

I must part with that little company I had. Here I parted from my daughter Mary, (whom I never saw again till I saw her in Dorchester, returned from captivity) and from four little cousins and neighbors, some of which I never saw afterward....

We traveled about half a day or a little more ... to this place, cold, and wet, and snowy, and hungry, and weary, and (only) the cold ground to sit on.... At this place we continued about four days.

Mary believed their fifth remove was caused by the English army, "it being near and following them. For they went as if they had gone for their lives.... In this travel I was somewhat favored in my load; I carried only my knitting work and two quarts of parched meal...."

From the eighth through the eighteenth remove, Mary ate ground nuts, bear meat, and even corn meal, but she was always hungry. She sewed shirts for Indian men and boys, which the Indian women did not know how to do. She saw her son again in one of the camps through which they passed and visited with him for a few hours.

Mary was assigned to work for an Indian woman named Weetamoo, who amused Mary by "dressing herself neat [ly] as much time as any of the gentry of the land; powdering her hair and painting her face, going with necklaces and jewels in her ears and bracelets upon her hands. When she had dressed herself, her work was to make girdles of wampum and beads."

Finally one of the Indian men told Mary that she was going to be released in two weeks' time. She was afraid to believe him, but she hoped with all her heart it was true.

When the letter was come, the sagamores met to consult about the captives, and called me to them to inquire how much my husband would give to redeem me....

They bid me speak what I thought he would give....
At a venture, I said "twenty pounds," yet desired them

to take less. But they would not hear of that, but sent that message to Boston, that for twenty pounds I should be redeemed....

Then Philip, smelling the business, called me to him and asked me what I would give him, to tell me some good news and speak a good word for me. I told him I could not tell what to give him, [that] I would give anything I had, and asked him what he would have. He said: two coats and twenty shillings in money, and half a bushel of seed corn and some tobacco. I thanked him for his love; but I knew the good news as well as the crafty fox....

On Tuesday morning they called their General Court (as they call it) to consult and determine whether I should go home or no. And they all as one man did seemingly consent to it, that I should be home, except Philip who would not come among them....

I was with the enemy eleven weeks and five days, and not one week passed without the fury of the enemy and some desolation by fire and sword upon one place or other....

But to return again to my going home, ... at first they were all against it, except my husband would come for me. But afterwards they assented to it and seemed much to rejoice in it. Some asked me to send them some bread, others some tobacco, others shaking me by the hand, offering me a hood and scarf to ride in — not one moving hand or tongue against it....

Mary parted company with the Wampanoags, escorted by one "Mr. Hoar," a man sent from Boston to arrange Mary's release, and two Indians. She soon rejoined her husband in Boston, "but the thoughts of our dear children, one being dead, and the others we could not tell where, abated our comfort each to [the] other," it would be about three months before the entire family was reunited. Young Joseph was released by the Indians when they were paid seven pounds ransom for him. Young Mary was released without any ransom being paid.

In August of that same year, King Philip was killed by colonists and the war ended. About two thousand settlers and four thousand Indians lost their lives in King Philip's War.

The Reverend Rowlandson moved his family to Withersfield, Connecticut, in 1677 when he was installed as pastor of a church there on April 7. He died of natural causes in November 1678, and the church officials awarded Mary a pension of 30 pounds a year.

Mary and her children moved back to Boston, where she wrote a book about her time spent in captivity. The book was published first in Cambridge, Massachusetts, in 1682, and later in London, England. It has since appeared in more than 30 editions and numerous anthologies.

The date of Mary's death is uncertain, but it was sometime after 1678.

Bibliography

Demos, John, ed. *Remarkable Providences 1600–1760.* New York: George Braziller, 1972, pp. 285–310.

Segal, Charles M., and David C. Stineback. *Puritans, Indians and Manifest Destiny.* New York: G. P. Putnam's Sons, 1977.

Vaughn, Alden T., and Edward W. Clark. *Puritans Among the Indians.* Cambridge, Mass.: Harvard University Press, 1981.

Williams, Selma R. *Dementer's Daughters.* New York: Atheneum, 1976.

22

Mary Barnard Williams

When the ship *Lyon* arrived in Boston on February 5, 1631, there were, in addition to the supplies being brought to the colonists, a number of passengers on board. Among them were Roger Williams and his wife, Mary, Margaret Winthrop, her stepson John Winthrop, Jr., and his wife, Martha. The ship had left England on December 10, 1630, and it had been a long, cold trip to the New World. These passengers had immigrated for religious freedom.

Roger Williams had been a Separatist for the past several years, and he said, "[Anglican] Bishop Laud pursued me out of the land."

It is uncertain where Roger and Mary stayed after they arrived in Boston, but it may have been with John Wilson, pastor of the newly formed church in Boston. Roger planned to serve as a teaching substitute for Wilson while the latter returned to England to bring his own wife to Boston. In fact, Roger delivered a few sermons for Wilson before the pastor left.

The Boston congregation liked Roger and his sermons, but he refused their invitation to be their regular teaching pastor because the church members would not renounce all their ties with the Church of England. Roger believed the Anglican Church was fatally flawed, even though his former classmate and good friend, John Winthrop, also a resident of Boston and a member of the congregation, retained his ties with the Church of England.

Roger was born about 1604 in London to a merchant tailor and his wife, James and Alice Pemberton Williams. Roger's father taught his three sons textile retailing, and after his arrival in Boston, Roger followed this line of work in addition to preaching.

Mary Barnard had married Roger on December 15, 1629, in England in the parish church at High Laver. She was 19 and Roger was about 25 years old.

Prior to her marriage Mary had been employed as a lady-in-waiting to Joan Altham, stepdaughter of one of Roger's society friends, Sir William Masham. Mary had little or no education and could not write. A friend of Roger's described her as modest, meek and patient, all qualities she would need in abundance during 45 years of marriage to Roger.

Shortly after their arrival, Roger made his displeasure known to John Winthrop, present governor of the Massachusetts Bay Colony, about Winthrop's continuing interest in the Church of England. Roger and Winthrop had attended Cambridge University at the same time and were friends of long standing.

Governor Winthrop advised Roger to be less noisy about his beliefs, but he had forgotten how determined Roger could be when he adopted a viewpoint.

In April 1631, Roger and Mary prepared to move to nearby Salem, where Roger had been invited to become an associate pastor. Winthrop warned Salem officials that Roger's ideas were radically different from theirs and suggested they withdraw their offer to him. Roger may have learned of Governor Winthrop's attempt to interfere, for he decided to bypass Salem and go to Plymouth.

Winthrop was glad to see Roger leave Boston. He feared the theocratic form of government in Boston could not withstand bitter, protracted controversy, and he judged Roger to be a potential troublemaker. Winthrop's fortune was invested in the success of the Boston colony, and he could not afford to have it fail.

In Plymouth, Roger found believers who were more attuned to

his beliefs than the people in Boston had been. The worshippers in Plymouth had unofficially separated from the Anglican Church many years before, and worship was based entirely on their interpretations of scriptural teachings.

The Plymouth congregation still missed their beloved pastor, John Robinson, still in Leyden, Holland. They had been trying to save enough money to pay his passage to the New World, but the challenge was proving too great.

The Reverend Ralph Smith was the pastor of the congregation when Williams arrived, but few really like him. Roger, a fervent, charismatic speaker, served as a teaching pastor for about two years.

It was while Roger and Mary lived in Plymouth that Roger decided to begin studying Dutch and some of the Indian dialects with the idea of becoming a missionary to the Indians.

Plymouth citizens could not afford to pay their preachers much money, and Roger was not an exception. As he recorded in his diary, he had to work "day and night, at home and abroad, on the land and water, at the hoe, at the oar for bread." He did, however, take time to begin his missionary efforts with the Indians.

Then Roger became a concern for his Plymouth brethren. They felt he had added meddling to his preaching by writing a document that he circulated among them, questioning the right of the king of England to grant patents or charters for settlement by anyone anywhere in New England or other locations in the New World. Roger insisted all the land really belonged to the Indians, and that English officials had no more right to give away titles to Indian property than the Indians would have to give away property in England.

The lack of an official patent or charter for the Plymouth colony had long concerned the people of Plymouth. Governor Bradford and other officials felt Roger's actions could be dangerous to the very survival of the colony.

Edward Winslow was one of the few Plymouth founders who

wondered uneasily whether Roger could be correct. Some of the church members, speaking of Williams, said scornfully that "God had put a windmill in his head," and Governor Bradford agreed that Roger had "formed some strange opinions."

Deacon Cushman had expressed the opinion in 1622 that it was the Englishman's duty to convert the Indians, writing, "Now it seemeth unto me that we ought also to endeavor ... to convert them. ... Since to us they cannot come, our land is full; to them we may go; their land is empty.... So is it lawful now to take a land which none useth and make use of it?"

Plymouth citizens had accepted Cushman's statement, traded with the Indians as fairly as they knew, and did pay them for the land they occupied. Other colonists in the region, however, were not as honest.

One of the ways some of the dishonest settlers managed to acquire land the Indians were "not using" was by allowing their cattle to trample Indian crops repeatedly, destroying them. Any fences the Indians built to protect their property were mysteriously torn down, and at last the Indians would move away from their tormentors, "abandoning their land." Other dishonest colonists got the Indian men drunk and then tricked them into signing deeds that they could not read. Even some government officials in Massachusetts set fines for misdeeds so high the Indians could not possibly pay them. Then a generous white settler would come forward and offer to buy the Indian's land to "help out."

Roger and Mary Williams began to feel they had lost favor with the Plymouth colonists, and they left a short time later to go to Salem.

In Salem, the couple felt they had found a real home. A year after Roger had accepted the post of assistant to the pastor of the Salem church, the pastor died of tuberculosis, and Roger became the full-time pastor. Boston authorities protested Roger's appointment, but Salem church officers ignored Boston's advice.

The years Mary and Roger lived in Salem would be some of the happiest of their lives. Mary enjoyed living in the larger house provided there, which had formerly been the home of a Salem teacher. The Williamses' first child, a daughter named Mary, was born in Salem.

Roger was working harder than ever, delivering two long sermons each Sunday, as well as three regular weekday sermons. He also farmed, traveled in connection with his textile trading business, and continued his ministry among the Indians nearby.

As Governor Winthrop suspected, Roger did march to the beat of a different drummer than the other colonists. When Roger was eight years old, he had seen men burned at the stake in England for their Separatist beliefs, and the sight made a profound impression on the little boy. He reasoned that if these men were willing to die for their beliefs, they must be right.

At Cambridge University both Roger and Winthrop were dissidents of the Anglican Church. But John Winthrop had no intention of ever breaking with the Church as long as he thought it might be reformed.

Roger had also not tempered his arguments that had led him and Mary to leave Plymouth and move to Salem. He continued to insist the colonists had no legal right to the land they occupied, and some of his followers even questioned Governor Winthrop's authority to govern in the area of Massachusetts.

This challenge could not go unanswered. Governor Winthrop had Roger arrested and brought to Boston to stand trial for advocating the destruction of the civil government.

Roger had added a new twist to his arguments that civil government and church governments should be two separate entities, with neither having any control over the other. At this time in Massachusetts, the law stated that "no man shall be admitted as a freeman, to the freedom of the body politic, but such as are members of some of the churches within the same." Roger could not understand why a member or members of one group should decide who would be or not be a member of the other group. Winthrop could not understand why Roger could not agree that good men of wealth and education should be in control of both church and state governments, because, Winthrop reasoned, the poorer classes had no knowledge or experience in governing.

Mary, who disagreed with Roger that church members should separate from the Anglican Church, wanted to stay in Salem. She was pregnant again and was getting tired of moving from place to place. Roger was so hurt by her opposition that he refused to pray with her, refusing even to say grace before meals when she was at the table. Most of their friends and acquaintances pitied Mary.

Mary knew she could not continue to argue with him, so she finally agreed that their fellow colonists were all in error and Roger was right.

After much wrangling and disputing between Roger and his critics, on October 9, 1635, Roger was ordered by the General Court to leave the Salem area with his family by spring. Probably the only reason he received this much leniency was because of Mary's pregnancy. Their second child, whom they named Freeborn, was born several weeks later.

In December of that year, Massachusetts Bay officials discovered that Roger was continuing to hold religious gatherings in his home while he waited to leave Salem. The officials decided to deport him at once. Roger claimed later he was forced to place a mortgage on his home and land in Salem to get the money to pay for their move.

When the officials went to arrest Roger at his home, they found he had left Salem three days earlier to search for a place where he could take his family to live. Mary and their children were waiting until he could come back for them.

Years later, it was learned that Governor Winthrop had sent a timely warning to his old school friend that he faced imminent deportation, telling Roger he should leave Salem immediately. Winthrop had reason to fear that if Roger returned to England, he would either be imprisoned for the rest of his life or put to death.

Roger was sick when he left his Salem home, and if it had not been for the shelter and nursing provided him by his kind Indian friends, he would likely have died during the following weeks of bitter cold and snowy weather.

About the middle of April 1636, Roger reached what is now Rhode Island and founded the town of Providence. Some of his friends and followers joined him there and built homes for their families.

Roger had influenced the colonists in Plymouth more than he knew. About the time he reached Rhode Island in 1636, the Plymouth town government was reorganized and the rules for citizenship had changed. Any man who lived regularly in Plymouth, who had a family and pledged his allegiance to the town government, could vote for town officers, whether he belonged to a church or not.

When Mary Williams brought their children from Salem to join Roger in 1637, she found a village had already sprung up around his teachings. He had established a trading post in what would become Wickford.

Other colonists left Massachusetts Bay and moved to Rhode Island in 1638, among them William Coddington and William and Anne Hutchinson. In the spring of 1639, Coddington and the Hutchinsons laid out a new village, which was named Portsmouth, a short time later. Coddington was elected judge of the little village, and his judgeship represented the only form of government the village had.

These people soon disagreed sharply among themselves, and William Hutchinson became the new judge. Coddington left Portsmouth and moved on with some supporters to another section of the island where they founded Newport.

Roger Williams continued to visit Indian villages frequently and sometimes brought Indians home with him. Mary did not always share his enthusiasm for the Indian visitors, but she did not argue and she fed them from whatever small store of food she had. With their increasing family, food was often scanty.

Their house in Rhode Island was undoubtedly much like those in Plymouth, but it was smaller, with only one large room, similar to the other houses in early Rhode Island.

Mary and Roger's family continued to increase to a total of six children: Mary, Freeborn, Joseph, Providence, Mercy and Daniel. When Edward Winslow came from Plymouth to pay a visit, he was inwardly shocked to see how pitifully destitute the Williams family was. Before he left, Edward gave Mary a gold piece to help buy supplies for their new home.

Roger Williams lost some of his influence as the Rhode Island area attracted more settlers. The Quakers founded a strong colony nearby. No one persecuted them for their beliefs, but Roger did not agree with some of their ideas and practices, one of which was allowing women to be speakers in their meetings. He insisted only men should be designated "apostles," according to Corinthians.

Roger returned to England with physician John Clarke to obtain confirmation of the charter for Providence, Warwick and Aquidneck Island in the Rhode Island area. While there he wrote a treatise entitled *Experiments of Spiritual Life and Health*, primarily for Mary's guidance.

The charter for Rhode Island was sealed on July 8, 1663, at Whitehall. It was said Rhode Island was a colony of liberty without law, and Massachusetts Bay was a colony of law without liberty. Church governments and civil government had no interaction in Rhode Island.

Roger found himself defending his Indian friends again when he insisted the cattle grazing rights Indians granted settlers in Rhode Island did not include ownership of the land.

Mary Williams died in 1674, two years before an Indian attack destroyed most of the homes in Providence. Due to Roger's teachings and the Quakers' opposition to violence, there were few defenses, and two years later the towns of Warwick and Providence were destroyed by Indians. Roger's house was burned, as well as all his paper and books.

Roger Williams lived until 1683, probably dying at the home of a son, with whom he had been living since Mary's death.

Bibliography

Covey, Cyclone. *The Gentle Radical, Roger Williams.* New York: Macmillan, 1966.

Elliott, Emory, ed. *American Colonial Writers, 1606 to 1734.* Detroit: Gale Research, 1984.

Garrett, John. *Roger Williams.* London: Macmillan, 1970.

23

Margarethe Bechtel Jungmann

Margarethe Bechtel came to America with her parents and two older sisters seeking religious freedom. Her mother had been exiled from her native France earlier because of her adherence to the Reformed faith, but her father had not fully determined which religious group most nearly reflected his own beliefs.

Margarethe was born in Frankenthal, Germany, on September 13, 1721, where her father, Johannes Bechtel, worked as a master woodcrafter. The little girl was baptized in the Reformed Church, in accordance with her mother's beliefs.

Mr. Bechtel, on hearing good reports about life in America, decided to move his family to the Pennsylvania area. They arrived in fall of 1726.

Mr. Bechtel bought land and a house in Germantown near Philadelphia, and the girls were educated at home, learning to read the Bible, hymnbooks and the book *True Christianity*, by Johannes Arndt.

In 1741 Count Nicholas Ludwig von Zinzendorf came to preach in Philadelphia, and Margarethe was impressed by the evident strength of his religious convictions. He had become the leader of a religious group known as the Renewed Church of United Brethren in Europe. Because of their location in the province of Moravia, they became known as Moravians in America.

The count's theology was based on heartfelt, rather than reasoned, beliefs. He believed God was revealed to mankind by his Son, the Christ, and all the rules people needed to live a righteous life could be found in the Bible. He encouraged both men and women members of his congregations to write their memoirs as a way to keep alive their past with their friends, and also to keep a record of the history of the church.

When Count Zinzendorf established a children's school in Germantown, Margarethe became acquainted with some of the younger members of the Moravian faith. Among them were the count's sister, Anna Nitschmann, and his daughter, Benigna. They and Margarethe became friends.

In the spring of 1741, Count Zinzendorf had the first log cabin built to start a village for his followers called Bethlehem in the Pennsylvania colony. The members of his Moravian congregation made the village their communal home and later moved the school to Bethlehem.

From the time the members moved into Bethlehem, during the period from 1742 to 1762, everything in the village was owned in common — land, houses, and even businesses. Women lived in groups called choirs with other women — even, at first, those who were married — and men lived in choirs with other men. If married couples had children, the babies were taken to live in the "Nurserie" after they were weaned.

Apparently some members complained about the arrangement, and after 1762 only unmarried women and widows lived in choirs, as did the bachelors and widowers. Families lived together in their own household after that time.

When the school moved to Bethlehem, Margarethe was saddened that her friends had moved away, so her mother took her to visit in Bethlehem. They were present at the Holy Communion service while there, and Margarethe decided she wanted to join the congregation.

Count Zinzendorf wrote Mr. Bechtel, telling him of Margarethe's desire and saying he believed she belonged with the congregation. Mr. Bechtel reacted sharply, ordering Margarethe to return home at once with her mother. They did as he asked.

As Margarethe wrote in her *Memoirs*, "A few weeks later, the Count traveled to Germantown again and spoke with my father personally, and gave himself great pains on my behalf, but he had to use quite serious arguments to persuade him...."

The officials of the Moravian Church during this time exerted extraordinary control over the lives of their members by telling them where they should live, what job they should take, whom they should marry and how to rear their children.

Some members were assigned to do mission work so new members could be added to their numbers. They would have possibly had greater success sooner if the officials of the church had not insisted on speaking German.

Margarethe recorded in her *Memoirs* the events of her early days with the congregation: "I was immediately received into the Congregation and soon attained to the Holy Communion. I had hardly been here a couple of months when a proposal of marrying my first husband, the late Br. Buttner, who was then the preacher in Tolpehoken was made to me.... I was immediately willing to accept and we were married by the late Disciple [Count Zinzendorf]. A few days later, it was decided that we should go among the Indians at Schekomeko."

Located in Duchess County in northern New York, Schekomeko was the first mission to the Mohican Indian tribe by Moravian believers.

Margarethe felt inadequate to the task of winning converts because she was not sure of her own beliefs at times, but she went, determined to try.

A passage from her *Memoirs* reflects her anguish: "In my parents' house I had everything I wanted. Now I found myself placed in a situation of the utmost poverty. Many a day we hardly knew where we should find something to eat.... But I learned the language of the

Indians very quickly and soon gained a love for them and was loved by them in return, and this cheered me up again and made my course … easier."

Margarethe and her husband had been working with the Mohican tribe about three years when Mr. Buttner died of tuberculosis on February 23, 1745. Margarethe was then six months pregnant with their first child. On March 1 of that year, she returned to Bethlehem with fellow Moravians, and her son was born there in June. The baby, however, died when he was only three weeks old, and Margarethe found her faith tested by these two tragedies that had followed so closely upon each other.

She married a second time on August 24, 1745, to Johann Georg Jungmann, and they went to work in the Children's School in Frederickstown. A year later a daughter was born to them.

When the baby was three months old, Margarethe and her husband were called to Gnadenhutten, in Ohio, to serve an Indian Congregation of the Delaware tribe known as the Lenni Lenape. There the Jungmanns worked for the next six years.

They moved back to Bethlehem for several months before receiving a call to Pachgatgoch in New York state to work with Indians there. This mission location neighbored the Schekomeko mission, and they could visit with old friends. They remained in this location for three and a half years, during the last weeks of which the French and Indian War began; they returned to Bethlehem once more.

During these years Margarethe became proficient in speaking the Delaware and Mohican Indian languages. She also became pregnant ten times and had seven more children.

The Jungmann family worked for the next 18 months on a communal farm in Christiansbrunn, and then returned to Bethlehem, where they worked for the next nine years making soap for the fellow members of the congregation.

Moravian brothers and sisters were assigned jobs as well as missionary duties. Some worked cutting trees, tending livestock or doing any other work necessary in exchange for food, housing, education, medical care and even clothing for their families and themselves. In their *oeconomie*—a system wherein the community's goods are shared—members were allowed to keep money they had brought with them, but it had to be deposited with the *oeconomie* directors.

Bethlehem was one of the largest Moravian settlements in America during the 1700s, but there were also Nazareth and Letitz in Pennsylvania. Others such as Bethabara, Bethenia and Salem were in the North Carolina colony, and some smaller ones were located in New Jersey. Others were in New York, Ohio and Maryland.

When the Jungmanns were called to serve at Wihilusing, in Pennsylvania along the Susquehanna River, Margarethe was ordained as a deaconess before they left Bethlehem. After serving a year and half there, they were sent to Languntotenunk, also in Pennsylvania.

Eighteen months later they went to another mission station of the Delaware tribe at Muskingum, situated along the river of the same name, and remained here for five years. Their children had grown up and were in homes of their own by now.

They were serving in the Ohio mission of Lictenau when the Revolutionary War began between American and British forces. The Delawares and Moravians tried to remain neutral but soon the Jungmanns were forced to return to Bethlehem.

After three years there, Brother David Zeisberger came to visit them, and he asked them to go with him back to the Indian mission at Schoenbrunn.

As Margarethe wrote in her *Memoirs*,

> We were also willing and ready to venture there again, trusting in the help of the dear Saviour and in the hope of concluding our lives with the dear Indian Congregation, to which I felt a particularly strong attachment. Brother Reichel, who was here as a Visitor at that time, encouraged us to do this and we thus set off on the journey with the blessing of the Congregation. It was June

8th, 1781, and on July 12th we arrived at Schoenbrunn, to our joy and that of the dear Indian Congregation....

But we were hardly there for six weeks when the greatest crisis came — we were all taken prisoner and the three Indian Congregations were destroyed. That was hard and painful for us.

Some Indian tribes had aided the British invaders, but the Delawares had not.

After their release, the Jungmanns moved to Detroit, settling by the Huron River. They ministered to the Indians there for three years, until Margarethe's health failed and she told her husband she was too sick to stay at the mission location.

All the stress and anxiety of the past few years had taken their toll on Margarethe. She and her husband left, heading back to Bethlehem, where they arrived on November 22, 1785. There their daughter, Susanna, cared for her mother during her final illness.

Margarethe died at midnight on November 22, 1793, with several family members and neighbors present. She was 72 years old and had been married to Brother Jungmann for 48 years.

All her children survived her except the son who died in infancy and one daughter, who died several years before her mother on the island of Saint Thomas where she was also serving as a missionary.

The Moravian Church is active and thriving today, with about 165 congregations in North America and about 100,000 members. Worldwide there are approximately 450,000 members in about 500 congregations.

Bibliography

Davis, Chester. *Hidden Seed and Harvest: A History of the Moravians.* Winston-Salem, N.C.: Wachovia Historical, 1959.

Faull, Katherine M. *Moravian Women's Memoirs, Their Related Lives 1750–1820.* Syracuse: Syracuse University Press, 1997.

Josephy, Alvin M., Jr. *The Indian Heritage of America.* New York: Alfred A. Knopf, 1968.
Kirkland, Winifred. *The Easter People.* New York: Fleming H. Revell, 1923.
Pomfret, John E. *Colonial New Jersey: A History.* New York: Fleming H. Revell, 1923.
Restad, Penne L. *Christmas in America.* New York: Oxford University Press, 1995.
Thorp, Daniel B. *The Moravian Community in North Carolina.* Knoxville, Tenn.: University of Tennessee Press, 1989.

Index